Stanley Ketchel
A Life of Triumph and Prophecy

Manuel A. Mora

authorHOUSE®

AuthorHouse™
1663 Liberty Drive
Bloomington, IN 47403
www.authorhouse.com
Phone: 1-800-839-8640

This book is a work of non-fiction. Unless otherwise noted, the author and the publisher make no explicit guarantees as to the accuracy of the information contained in this book and in some cases, names of people and places have been altered to protect their privacy.

© 2010 Manuel A. Mora. All rights reserved.

No part of this book may be reproduced, stored in a retrieval system, or transmitted by any means without the written permission of the author.

First published by AuthorHouse 10/21/2010

ISBN: 978-1-4343-2370-5 (sc)

Library of Congress Control Number: 2007907386

Printed in the United States of America

This book is printed on acid-free paper.

Because of the dynamic nature of the Internet, any Web addresses or links contained in this book may have changed since publication and may no longer be valid. The views expressed in this work are solely those of the author and do not necessarily reflect the views of the publisher, and the publisher hereby disclaims any responsibility for them.

Contents

Chapter 1:   Saturday, October 15, 1910 1
Chapter 2:   Beginnings and Recollections 5
Chapter 3:   Chicago and Socker Flanagan 9
Chapter 4:   Butte Montana and the Ring Debut 14
Chapter 5:   Ketchel vs. Tommy Ryan and California 31
Chapter 6:   Thomas vs. Ketchel I 41
Chapter 7:   Thomas vs. Ketchel II 48
Chapter 8:   Thomas vs. Ketchel III 53
Chapter 9:   Ketchel and the Sullivan Brothers 67
Chapter 10: Papke, Kelley and, once again, Thomas 92
Chapter 11: Ketchel Knocks Out Four Heavyweights
             in one Night 104
Chapter 12: Ketchel vs. Papke II 108
Chapter 13: Ketchel vs. Papke III 115
Chapter 14: Ketchel vs. Caponi and O'Brien 121
Chapter 15: Ketchel vs. O'Brien II 131
Chapter 16: Ketchel vs. Papke IV 136
Chapter 17: Ketchel vs. Johnson 142
Chapter 18: Wilson Mizner, Franz Klaus and Sam Langford 149
Chapter 19: Ketchel vs. Flynn, Lewis and Smith 157
Chapter 20: Walter and Goldie 163
Chapter 21: October 16, 1910 - The Capture 178
Chapter 22: The Funeral - A Touching Send Off 183
Chapter 23: Walter and Goldie on Trial 187
Chapter 24: The Prophecy: "I won't live to be 30!" 203
The End 219

Chapter 1:
Saturday, October 15, 1910

On October 15, 1910, Middleweight Boxing Champion of the World, Stanley Ketchel, was nearing the end of his daily jog on the dirt roads of the Missouri Ozarks. He was soaked from head to toe from a rain that began falling as he approached the country ranch where he was training. Ketchel loved the great outdoors. Every morning at six o'clock, he entered the crisp Ozark air and jogged fourteen miles to build his stamina. Both inside of the boxing ring and out, if there was one thing that defined Ketchel, it was stamina. From his electrifying bouts to his boundless personality, stamina was his stronghold.

After finishing his run and changing clothes, Ketchel had an appetite for breakfast. As he ate his eggs and grits, he watched the sun break through the clouds and illuminate the sprawling ranch's green terrain. He felt like he belonged there. The natural scenery calmed his mind and he was able to train and regain his health without distraction. The "camp", as Ketchel called it, was a stone's throw away from Conway, Missouri, and roughly forty-five miles from Springfield.

Manuel A. Mora

How Ketchel—a long time resident of the Grand Rapids, MI.—ended up in the Missouri countryside was a matter of personal connections: the ranch was owned by millionaire sportsman, "Colonel" R.P. Dickerson, who had been friends with Ketchel's mother during their childhood in Michigan. After learning that her eldest son was a boxer, Dickerson—ever the sportsman—became interested in Ketchel's career. After learning of Ketchel's ambitions and convincing Ketchel that he could help him, Dickerson sent word to the staff at his ranch that Ketchel would be arriving on September 15th, 1910. When he arrived at the ranch, Ketchel was far from an inexperienced boxer that harbored dreams of contention. He had already fought and lost to Jack Johnson, and he was looking to add weight to his 158-pound frame in preparation for a rematch with the champ.

Dickerson promptly introduced Ketchel to Springfield society and invited him to join the Elks Club. Within weeks, Ketchel was a popular figure on Springfield's social scene, and not least for his purported eccentricity. During his early morning runs, he could often be seen jogging with Dickerson's pet lion cubs, grasping their diamond studded leashes as he ran. Ketchel soon became as taken with Springfield as Springfield was with him; so much so that he decided to make the town his home. After finalizing his decision, he composed two letters: one to his parents in Michigan and another one to a friend in the Bronx:

> September 18th 1910
> Springfield, MO
>
> Springfield, Missouri is my place now. It is the best country in the world and I have tried them all and I know. I have quit the fighting game and I'm going into the farming business. I have bought 32,000 acres of timberland and 800 acres of the best farming land in the world. I intend to incorporate for about $300,000, put it in a sawmill and

lumber it off. It will give me one of the finest farms in the world. If I do anymore fighting, it will be for charity. This is the place for me to settle down, raise a family, raise animals and go to church every Sunday. Write to me with all the news and give my best to Willie Lewis, one of the best little fellows in the world.

Your farmer pal,
Stanley
Lumber President

Contrary to his letter, Ketchel planned to fight again as Middleweight Champion. He had been offered $30,000—a tremendous sum in 1910—to fight the black heavyweight, Sam McVey, in Paris, France. Ketchel wired his former trainer, Pete "The Goat" Stone, in New York: *"Get trunks ready for the trip and get reservations ready for the trip"*, were Ketchel's orders. In the meantime, since Ketchel needed experience in the timber business before striking out on his own, Dickerson agreed to let him take charge of his ranch while he was briefly away on business. While there, Ketchel would also train for his fight with McVey. Before Dickerson left the ranch on October 13th, he hired ranch hands and housekeepers to assist Ketchel.

Arriving at the ranch on Thursday morning without realizing what lay ahead of him, Ketchel said good morning to the ranch hands and headed toward the rear of the ranch house. He opened the screen door and entered the kitchen. The new cook was preparing his breakfast, and he remarked on how delicious the food smelled. The ranch cook, a woman of 19, looked at the smiling champion with eyes that were deliberately expressionless.

Before Ketchel left the kitchen, she replied in an indifferent tone, "I'll set your breakfast in the dining room. It'll be ready in a moment."

Ketchel headed toward the washstand in the east dining room. But just as he was freshening up for breakfast, Walter Dipley, a troublesome ranch hand that had once threatened Ketchel's life, was walking toward the house. After washing up, Ketchel put on a fresh shirt and parted his hair to the side. He smiled at himself in the mirror, noting with satisfaction the improved color in his face and how his arms had gotten thicker from training. But Ketchel was riding high on more than his looks. His upcoming fight with McVey would be his first trip out of the United States to defend his title. Ketchel thought the trip would be a good experience for him, for he had never left the States. In his excitement over his fight with McVey, he even announced to the boxing world that, if he failed to get another match with Jack Johnson, he would officially retire. Figuring that he would defeat McVey, Ketchel intended for his announcement to set boxing promoters scrambling to schedule a Ketchel/Johnson rematch, lest the opportunity pass them by.

After freshening up, Ketchel walked back to where the cook had laid his breakfast plate. As he questioned he about why there was only one chair at the table, she muttered inaudibly and tossed his utensils on the table. Ketchel sat down in the lone chair, his back facing the kitchen door just behind him. As Ketchel seemed to suspect, the single chair and its positioning was a set-up, for just as he was slicing into his steak, Dipley stealthily opened the door and crept up behind him.

Ketchel, always superstitious and devoted to self-protection, had unholstered his blue .45 six-shooter and set it on his lap prior to Dipley's entrance. Too involved in his breakfast to sense the danger that lay behind him, Ketchel was a sitting duck. From just a few feet away, Dipley aimed a .22 caliber rifle at Ketchel's back. Gripping the stock tight, he pulled the trigger and fired.

Chapter 2:
Beginnings and Recollections

On September 14th, 1886, Stanislaus Steven Kiecal (Ketchel's Christian name) was born on the Westside of Grand Rapids, Michigan, into a hard working family. His father, Thomas Kiecal, had immigrated to Michigan from Polish Prussia and found work in the Witticomb furniture factory. His mother, Julia, was born in Grand Rapids to Polish parents and was a homemaker. Years later, in 1909, Ketchel recounted his familial beginnings a little differently:

> I was born at Butte, Montana on September 14, 1887, and not in Grand Rapids, Mitch, in 1886 as the record books have it. My father is a native of Russia and my mother Slav. She was married when she was 13 years old and I was her first child, born a year after my parents' marriage. My mother's maiden name is Olbrisky and her mother was a full-blooded native of Poland. I have four other brothers.

The Twelfth Census of the United States confirms Ketchel's 1886 birth-date in Grand Rapids. His mother was 14 and his father was 32. The Kiecals would soon have other children. John was born in June of 1889; Alexander was born February of 1892 and Leonard was born in March of 1894. A fifth child would follow later—a half-brother named Arthur. Ketchel was only 11 when he went to work polishing furniture in Witticomb furniture factory, earning four dollars a week. Ketchel described his mood around this time as follows:

> After a little schooling at Grand Rapids, when I attended St. Aldalbert's School and one year at Union High School, I went to work for $4 a week, polishing furniture for the concern that employed my father. At the age of eleven I had worked so faithfully that I received the same salary as a man. But I began to get restless and I wanted to see the world.

Ketchel's adolescent restlessness was soon getting him into trouble around the neighborhood, especially after he became the leader of a "kid" gang called the West Sides. With calloused palms and no illusions about what lay ahead of them in life, they were roustabouts with a penchant for orneriness; who scrapped among themselves and with anyone that they could goad into fighting. In his self-published biography of Ketchel, The Michigan Assassin, Nat Fleischer describes how Ketchel laughed uproariously during a 1909 interview while discussing his childhood and the trouble it caused his father:

> There's no use getting away with. I was a tough kid who needed walloping and I got what was coming to me every time Dad socked me. The funny thing about it is that the old man was secretly proud of my being able to lick a lot of bigger chaps than myself. He never said so in so many words, but he gave himself away because every time I got a licking from him, an hour or so later, he would slip me

a dime, at the same time threatening me if I misbehaved again. He was true blue, was the old man, and when I got to be Champ, he couldn't have been more pleased than if I had been made the President of the United States. Grand Rapids had nothing to offer as far as making a living. The older I got the more I wanted to leave."

The young Ketchel left home in 1899. Some sources put his age of departure at 15, but he was actually 13. Ketchel's primary reason for leaving home was that his absence would improve his parents' impoverished state, although some historians suggest that he left because he wanted to see what was left of the American West, which is true in part, and is based on an article written by Arthur Ketchel for a September 1961 issue of *Boxing Illustrated*, in which Arthur says: "There are a few mistakes always written about the way he started as a fighter. The truth is that he decided to leave Michigan and go out West and be a cowboy."

It is true that Ketchel did not originally intend to be a boxer; he wanted to be a cowboy. But the catalyst for his leaving home was a sympathetic awareness of his family's needs. At the age of 12, he convinced his "little mother," Julia, that he should leave home to find his fortune. He would return home, he said, only after he had realized a level of success that would allow him to support his family. With his mother's begrudging permission to leave home, Ketchel and his friend, Tommy Desland, left in the spring of 1899 for the Western United States. Desland, also known as "Cuba" for having lived in Havana as a child, was proud that Ketchel had chosen him for his traveling companion. In addition to being an experienced traveler, the 15-year-old Desland was the oldest member of Ketchel's West Side gang.

Ketchel and Desland spent the next two years wandering across the Midwest, sleeping in freight trains, riding on the underside of boxcars and running from railroad officers, who in many cases were more brutal than the criminals that the boys encountered in hobo jungles where they occasionally made camp. For Ketchel, life in the hobo jungles was both an adventure and a quest for survival. Little did he know that he was camping in the underbelly of a lawless era of American history where desperate men were known to kill each other for not much.

In December 1901, Ketchel and Desland hopped a freight train bound for Detroit. As they neared the outskirts of the city, they combined their money and found that it amounted to a mere 30 cents. But Tommy had an older sister living in Detroit, and in a few days she would give him two dollars to help them on their way. With the money in hand, the boys made plans to travel to Chicago and find work. As The Westbound Flyer pulled out of the railroad yards, the boys dove inside one of its freight cars and settled down for a long ride, but an ill-fated run-in with a railroad policeman would shatter their plans.

In the early 20th century, trains regularly stopped a short distance from their destination so that railroad officers could inspect the cars for hobos. Suddenly, The Westbound Flyer began slowing to a halt in the early morning darkness, and just before it stopped, a strapping, blackjack swinging railroad officer hopped into the car where Ketchel and Desland sat perplexed. The boys managed to skirt his attack and leap from the train. Tumbling to the ground, they gathered themselves and ran as fast as they could opposite the train's destination. But the officer was on their heels with his blackjack held high. Ketchel dodged to one side, changed his path and ran until he was hidden by the darkness, leaving the officer to chase Desland. In a few seconds, the train started moving again and Stanley resumed his former place in the freight car. Tommy had disappeared, and with him the two dollars. Ketchel was alone now, and his quest for survival in the hobo world was just beginning. A 13-year-old boy was about to experience the true meaning of the word "survival".

Chapter 3:
Chicago and Socker Flanagan

Ketchel arrived in Chicago penniless and with a bad reputation in tow. But instead of resuming his thieving ways, he journeyed to Van Buren Street to search for employment. With a growling stomach, finding a job fast was Ketchel's goal. Several hours had passed since he had last eaten, and as he looked up Van Buren Street, his attention gravitated toward a corner restaurant on the opposite side of the street. A few seconds after entering the restaurant, Ketchel met its proprietor, "Socker" Flanagan. Prior to becoming a businessman, Flanagan had been a boxer, fighting as a local lightweight and retaining a small fan base. After loosing his quick feet to age, he turned to the restaurant business and employed enough help to afford him a sense of retirement. Yet, with the kind of rough and tumble patronage that dined at his establishment, he constant presence was a necessity. Flanagan was lounging near the restaurant's entrance, smoking a cigar, when his attention was drawn to the approaching Ketchel. Years later, he would recall his initial impression of Ketchel:

I spotted him coming from a short distance, his appearance was disheveled, and worsened, yet, by the black filth from him riding the rails, all on his face, and tattered clothing... Here was this boy, clearly famished, looked as if he hadn't eaten in weeks, only weighing about 119 pounds, if that, and not more than 5'6" high. Ketchel come around the corner, then that's when he stepped upon Flanagan Street there where I could see him fully, another lad named Sweeny was sixteen, and much taller, heavier too. Sweeny was one tough young scrapper and the neighborhood he survived in, was tougher. Anyone who knew him expected him to have the upper hand in a fight with almost anyone close to his age, but here, this little urchin from out of no where tore into Sweeny so fast with such speed and rage, I could hardly believe my eyes.

Sweeny, Flanagan recalled, was dazed and bleeding from his nose and mouth when Ketchel was finished with him. Even though he started the fight, Sweeny was soon desperately trying to protect himself from Ketchel's quick punches. A crowd of onlookers had gathered to watch Sweeney fight. But to everyone's amazement, Sweeny backed away and bolted into the alley. Ketchel chased after him, but just as Ketchel rounded the corner, Flanagan grabbed him by the collar and pulled him inside the restaurant.

"There's a cop comin' down the block," warned Flanagan. "You don't wanna be put in the pen, do you? You should look at the sores and bruises on your face, boy. Ain't you had enough scrapping for today? How in the hell did you come to mix with Sweeny anyway?"

"He called me a filthy hobo!" Ketchel replied angrily.

Flanagan grinned as he examined Ketchel more closely. His face and hands were black with grime. His coat was as greasy, tattered and it was pocked with burn holes from hot the cinders that pelted him as he rode beneath freight cars. Ketchel's body was trembling and his voice was weak. He was literally starving, Flanagan observed, so he fed him right away.

"Well, just by lookin' at you kid, you don't look like a rough and tumble scrapper to me", Flanagan said. "But you sure got guts. Sweeny is big enough to put you to sleep with one punch. You don't belong around these parts. Where'd you come from?"

"I traveled on the Michigan Flyer from Detroit. I was traveling with a friend of mine, but thanks to a railroad cop he didn't make it here with me," Ketchel replied.

"I'm sorry about your buddy, and believe me, I know ridin' on the train ain't an easy trick," said Flanagan. "I did some of that rough ridin' myself when I was your age. I was young, and quite a bit more foolish. I have a wash stand in the back, better go back there; wash up, then you can throw a feed into you. I'm sure you haven't had a decent meal in weeks."

After Ketchel washed up and ate his meal, he conversed with Flanagan at length, revealing his desire to live in the open range of the American West as a cowboy. But the days of the Wild West had ended long ago, Flanagan pointed out.

"All that stuff about Indians and train robbers is history. Them days is over," Flanagan explained. "I gotta say though, there are plenty of tough miners around that act pretty free with six-shooters. Now, the cowboys are mostly a hard working bunch of folks that live peaceful lives, except when they hit this here town for a good time after payday. You better believe it, though; them minin' camps are rough spots. Anyway," Flanagan continued, "seeing as you're still the only kid here, don't you think you've got far enough West to lie up for a spell? Why don't you stick around and work for me for a spell? I could use you around the joint. I have an idea you won't settle down for long! You've got the wander bug, and you're sure 't hit the road again someday. I was the same, wanderin' just myself when I was your age."

Flanagan persuaded Ketchel to take a job in his 24-hour restaurant. Alternating between day and evening shifts, Ketchel waited on customers and helped clean up after his shift ended. When business was slow, Flanagan introduced Ketchel to the art of glove-practice. Until then, Ketchel had never worn boxing gloves, but he took to glove practice with such efficiency that even Flanagan was amazed.

"For a little guy like you, I have to admit you carry a peach of a wallop," Flanagan commented. "You'll never be a Fancy Dan Fighter, there's too much slugging in you for that, but when you're older and put on weight, I'm thinking you'll go far in the ring if you take that way of making a living, and why not? There's no better business on earth for a chap that's got a punch and the heart to take it. You could be a real champion one day with the dollars rollin' in and the newspaper guys printin' your picture, writin' all kinds of guff about you."

Flanagan mostly made his prediction to inspire Ketchel, but he would be a truer prophet than he anticipated. Ketchel's professional boxing debut was still years away. But by meeting Flanagan and rubbing shoulders with the sports fanatics that patronized his restaurant, Ketchel's mind was increasingly on boxing instead of the Wild West.

Working at Flanagan's restaurant exposed Ketchel to the nuances of city life. As if symbolizing his passage from rural Michigan to Chicago, Ketchel followed Flanagan's suggestion to Americanize his name by changing it from Stanislaus Kiecal to Stanley Ketchel. No matter how you decide to make your way in life, Socker told Stanley, you'll benefit from not having a "foreign soundin'" name.

"You were born in America, so why carry a foreign brand?" questioned Flanagan. "Forget the Kiecal layout, and cop yourself a new handle: Ketchel. That's got more of a punch to it and is damn easy to curl your lip around."

Always ready to act on Flanagan's advice, Ketchel agreed to change his name. After changing his name, Ketchel remained in Chicago for two more years before his "wander bug" urged him on. Having made friends with Grant, an elder hobo who made a living wiring chairs, Ketchel took to the road once more at Grant's side. With Ketchel boring holes into the chairs and Grant wiring them, they made between eight to ten dollars a day as they traveled west, building a sizeable nest egg that would split when they parted company. But soon after they arrived in St. Paul, Minnesota, Grant mysteriously vanished with the money, leaving Ketchel dead broke. As before, he had no option but to ride the rails and navigate the dangerous hobo jungles.

Chapter 4:
Butte Montana and the Ring Debut

"I went further west working my way by harvesting and picking hops. I had a lot of hard experience during this roaming trip. I became a cowpuncher and learned to ride like a daredevil like the rest of the boys. – Stanley Ketchel, *New York Sun*, 1909

When Ketchel left Chicago, he was 14-years-old. Riding the rails was nothing new to him, and his past experiences with railroad officers and hobos kept him alert. Sometimes he would get lucky and find a place where he could sleep by himself. But on one such occasion, a police officer that was on the lookout for hobos on private property found him sleeping in an old barn and jailed him for the night. Upon arriving the police station, the police sergeant interrogated Ketchel and demanded to see his hands. Fortunately for Ketchel, his calloused hands indicated that he had been doing hard work, making the sergeant more sympathetic to his plight. The sergeant let him sleep in a cell and warned him to leave town at dawn. The next morning, Ketchel departed the jail and quickly jumped a freight train where he shared a car with other hobos. Based on his experience, Ketchel believed that there were different classes of hobos that ranged from good-natured to cutthroat, and that the hobos that surrounded him were of the latter type. He gave each of them a stern look to show he would not be easy prey.

Ketchel was glad he had gotten a full night's sleep at the jail; it allowed him stay awake and alert in the midst his companions. He had felt uneasy as their eyes followed him to his initial place in the car, so he decided to move near the car's door. If one of the hobos approached him, they would literally find themselves hopping the rails. And if they tried to "gang" him, he'd hop off himself.

Heading west on the rails, Ketchel was bound for Barnsville, Minnesota, where ranch hands were in demand. As expected, the train halted just short of its destination and railroad officers banished the hobos, swinging black jacks as they went. After being kicked from a train, hobos would spend most of their time hopelessly panhandling and searching for food. But since Ketchel was smaller and better looking than the rest of the hobos that day, he had little trouble getting handouts. The Barnesville housewives secretly gave him the most cakes and sandwiches.

Leaving the other hobos behind, Ketchel walked to a field on the outskirts of town and sat beneath a tree to eat. That night, he would journey further west by train toward Barnsville, where he would be hired to harvest crops and carry bundles for $2.50 a day. Within a matter of days, Ketchel was promoted to driving a tank wagon, and three weeks later he was made fireman of a threshing engine, raising his pay to $6 a day. Ketchel enjoyed the outdoor work and the three hearty meals a day. But after a few months of harvest, Ketchel found the fieldwork monotonous and journeyed to Winnipeg, were he was hired as a blacksmith's assistant in a railroad camp near Revelstroke. Ketchel had no blacksmithing experience, but told his bosses otherwise. The foreman—a sharp-tempered Scotsman that knew his trade well—soon discovered Ketchel's amateurism. Within two hours of arriving at the camp, Ketchel was running away from it as fast as he could, with the foreman on his tail and his co-workers cheering the race on. After easily outrunning the foreman, Ketchel headed toward Victoria. In his two hours as a blacksmith, he had heard about some mines near Victoria and decided to walk in that direction. On his way to the mines, he happened across a young Irishman who told him that he would need to be bigger to get a mining job.

"They wouldn't take me, and I'm several inches taller than you," said The Irishman.

Taking the man's advice, Ketchel opted to work in a sawmill in Arrowhead, riding logs. The work was grueling and the lodging was little better than a freight car. But the sawmill would be Ketchel's home for spell. As he rode logs in the bitter cold with just crumbs to eat, he vowed to return to Revelstroke to get revenge on those whom he felt had mistreated him. Planning for revenge, Ketchel stole a .22 Caliber rifle from a steamer captain and hid it in a lumber wagon. Before he returned to Revelstroke, he panned to fetch it and take it with him.

When Ketchel returned for the rifle, he forgot which wagon it was in and decided to search them all. Finally, he spied the rifle near the bottom of the wagon. The logs had slipped and were too heavy for him to move on his own, so he enlisted the help of another hobo. After retrieving the rifle, Ketchel and his new friend hid inside a toolbox beneath a freight train and made a 500-mile journey to Vancouver. After arriving in Vancouver and finding no work, Ketchel decided to journey 80 miles from Vancouver to the Ladysmith mines. He remembered the Irishman's words about being too small to work in the mines, but he was broke. Ketchel described his short experience at the mines and his trip back to Victoria in an interview with *Ring Magazine* creator, Nat Fleischer:

> Just as I was told previously, I was too small to get work in the mines and my application was refused to I started back for Victoria. I carried my 22. caliber rifle over my shoulder like a true hunter. I jumped aboard a freight train but shortly after I got the hitch, the train sidetracked on me and again I was on my own walking the tracks. I traveled on foot for I don't know how many miles, but I guess it was almost 180 miles. But, finally made Victoria.

While at Victoria, Ketchel's anger toward his situation at Revelstroke diminished, and he sold the rifle for $4 to pay for a steamer ticket to Seattle.

"When I reached Seattle it was freezing weather," Ketchel reported in the same interview with Fleischer. "The only way I could get food was to sell my surplus coats and vests, and in good hobo style, I wore one on top of the other. I didn't remain in Seattle for very long. I met a young fellow who seemed to know a few things about that part of the country and we skipped the city on another 'Blind Baggage.'"

With his renewed dream of becoming a cowboy in tow, Ketchel hopped a train headed for Montana. Contrary to Flanagan's advice, he still felt that the Wild West existed, just perhaps in a diminished state. When he reached Montana, he intended to join the wild riders of the open range, whose heroic acts had captured his imagination since childhood. Ketchel was riding in boxcar by himself—a rare luxury—and soon went to sleep. But when he awoke a few hours later, he didn't see the Montana range. All he saw was a few cracks of light outlining the closed door of the boxcar, and the car was sitting still in total silence. The car's doors had been locked from the outside and it sat discarded on a sidetrack. Ketchel interpreted the situation for what it was and began to panic. He had no way out, and he had heard stories of hobos starving to death in locked cars.

All Ketchel could do was scream at the top of his lungs and kick furiously at the door in hopes that someone would hear him. He knew that he was in rural surroundings, but he didn't know that the sidetrack was three miles away from the depot. Worse yet, the sidetrack that he was on was used to store broken cars for weeks or even years before they were taken to a repair yard.

Ketchel later said that the boxcar episode was the most horrifying event in his life. For two days, he was trapped without food and water, and his hands were bleeding from beating on the boxcar door. His voice had weakened to a hoarse whisper, and he was half mad from dehydration. He lay by the doors with his ear pressed close to a narrow fissure, hoping that he would hear a passerby. Amazingly, there came the sound of heavy feet along the tracks. Ketchel summoned his remaining strength, kicked furiously on the door and gave a shriek. The footsteps suddenly halted at the door. Ketchel heard the lock being unlatched. The door slid open and sunlight filled the car. A tall, stout man stood peered curiously into the car. For the first time in his life, Ketchel passed out.

When Ketchel came to, he was lying on a sofa in the home of a farmer named Edgar Landon, the man who had opened the boxcar. Having sympathy on Ketchel, Langdon carried him to his farmstead to nourish him back to health. Landon's elderly mother—a kind, matronly woman—was bending over Ketchel and holding a glass of wine to his lips when he awoke. The Landon's insisted that Ketchel spend the week with them, which he did. When he left, he promised to return one day—a promise that he kept when, after winning a championship and making a small fortune, he drove up to their house in a limousine loaded with gifts. In reminiscence, Ketchel described the Landon's as, "the two finest biggest hearted folks I ever knew!"

After Ketchel left the Landon's, he headed for Montana by freight train, and was careful not to fall asleep. When he arrived in Silver Bow, Montana, a brakeman told him to "hit the grit", which meant that he would have to walk the remaining seven miles to Butte. When he arrived in Butte at 16-years-old, he immediately fell in love with one of the wildest towns in the West. The Miners in Butte worked hard and played even harder. Race days, St. Patrick's Day, St. Georges Day, Miner's Union Day and election days were among the occasions that miners celebrated with passion and drunkenness, often gathering in Columbia Gardens—a trolley park on the east of town that had been built by William A. Clark. It offered picnic tables, a dance pavilion, concessions and playgrounds for children, as well as an establishment called, The Comique, which catered to more adult tastes, offering everything from Vaudeville to Burlesque.

Butte's red light district was said to compare to those of New Orleans and San Francisco, with some prostitutes earning as much as sixty dollars a night. Most of the women lived in cell-like apartments with a bed, a coal stove and a small dresser with a washbowl and pitcher. It was customary for each room's occupant to have her name emblazoned on the door. The prostitutes were usually paid in silver dollars, which they kept stashed in their stockings to prevent them from spilling out onto the street. "It was all they could do to navigate down the sidewalk," a man remarked near the turn of the century.

More than one hundred girls worked at the notorious Comique. One of its most famous tales involved a man known as Fat Jack Jones, who lost his false teeth after staking them in a poker game. "Fat Jack", as he was commonly called, went for nearly a week eating soup and other soft foods before he won his teeth back. Soon afterward, he ordered two steaks and ate them both.

Both Butte's mines and its "houses of ill repute" were going strong in 1902 when Ketchel arrived, and his first stop was at the back door of the famous Copper Queen—a hotel, café, saloon and whorehouse situated in the heart of town. The casino's proprietor, Josh Allen, opened the door, gave the clean cut Ketchel a once over, and invited him inside.

"You a cowhand?" Allen inquired of Ketchel. "Can you sling hash and hustle luggage?"

Ketchel nodded yes. "It don't sound too hard to me," he replied.

Allan hired Ketchel on the spot as a bellhop and put him to work immediately. Among Ketchel's other duties was carrying meals on trays to the nearest saloon two blocks away. In an issue of *Grand Rapids Herald*, Ketchel later described his adventures in the rough mining town:

> When I finally struck Butte my Native town, I got a job as a bellhop in a hotel. One day a fellow named Maurice Thompson became disorderly in the hotel and I had to make good before the boss, so I threw Thompson out bodily. He was something of a bully about town and posed a fighter. They raised a 25-dollar purse and asked me if I would meet Thompson for six rounds at the casino theater. This coin looked big to me then, and I quickly consented. But, I didn't know I was up against a braco game. They called the bout a draw after I had almost annihilated the bully and of course, I felt sore about it. I began to get wise right there. I was only 17 years old at the time and was naturally green at the fighting game. Oh yes, I fought many battles through Montana before and after I met Thompson, though I never kept any record of them, some were with cowpunchers, miners, and other fellows I ran up against during my travels. There were probably 250 battles that were never included in my ring record. I think my first fight was bare-knuckles

no holds-barred. It didn't last but two rounds, as I knocked him out without much trouble. I don't remember his name and I don't care. But, I know he was a grown man, while I was only a boy. After my go with Thompson the manager of the casino gave me a job meeting all corners at $20 a week. I used to answer bells at the hotel all day and fight all night, every night at the theater. I tell you that was damn pretty hard work and the punching I had to do in those days was certainly going some. There was a new fellow every night, and I had to put him away or lose my job. I use to fight with such rage and wallop them so hard that when they dropped the footlights would go out too. One night they matched me against a chap called the Marysville Kid. The manager hung up an 8-dollar purse for a ten round go. He told us that we had better split the money. I didn't like that so I walked over to the kid's corner to him. "I'll fight, winner take all," and just before the fight started the kid agreed. When the bell rang I got hot footed after the Marysville wonder and sent him to dreamland in the second round. When I went to collect my eight bones the manager objected but finally paid me in full after a red-hot argument. I've never since agreed to cut the money with any opponent for that sort of business always looks queer to me.

Ketchel would fight 250 amateur boxing matches in Butte, but none of them would help launch his professional career. However, in 1903, when he knocked out three drunken miners at the Copper Queen Casino, his luck began to change.

Late one night, the three bawdy miners entered The Copper Queen and headed toward the tables where an attractive Vaudeville actress named Goldie usually sat. Goldie was the prettiest girl in the casino and a seductive dancer on the stage. As the miners approached, she sat in her spangled stage dress, chatting with her boyfriend Joe, who worked as a bouncer. As the miners sat down and ordered drinks, Joe departed and a waiter stepped forward. It was the 17-year-old Ketchel. Ketchel fetched the miners' drinks and soon fetched them another round, and another and another. With each round, they grew increasingly aggressive toward Goldie, finally drawing Joe's attention. But before he could get to Goldie's table, one of the miners leaned forward and said something that caused Goldie to slap him. As the three miners jumped to their feet, Joe and Ketchel came forward and told them to pay up and leave. The miner that Goldie had slapped started protesting, and his two friends were soon moving in Joe's direction with clenched fists. But just as Joe was readying himself for a fight, he found Ketchel standing between him and the miners.

"This is my table; I'll take care of things," Ketchel whispered to Joe. Wanting his chance at chivalry, Joe was outraged at Ketchel's audacity. The miners sensed the antagonism between Joe and Ketchel, and oddly decided to stand behind Joe in opposition to Ketchel. Goldie stood silently against a nearby wall, fearing that Ketchel was about to get the beating of his life. Joe decided that he would first put Ketchel in his place and then handle the miners. He threw a fake left at Ketchel's head to throw him off balance and then tried to kick him in the groin. But Ketchel stepped aside, caught Joe's foot in his left hand and gave it a twist. With Joe off balance, Ketchel hit him in the nose with a crushing blow, knocking him unconscious. Then he turned to face the miners. Removing his waiter's apron as the crowd drew aside tables and chairs for the big showdown, Ketchel was observed laughing at the three miners. They were powerful, but they were also extremely drunk. As Ketchel leapt into action, he began maneuvering so that the miner's got in each other's way and had a hard time striking him. Suddenly, Ketchel leaped forward and hit one of the miners with a one-two combination to the jaw, pummeled him the stomach and quickly jumped back. Then he leapt forward and smashed another miner on the jaw. With the first two miners on the floor trying to gather their wits, the third began shielding his face, making it easy for Ketchel to pound him in the stomach, which left him doubled up on the floor.

Neither the miners nor Joe wanted a second go around with Ketchel. Having just watched a wiry, 17-year-old boy lay out four strong men in less a minute, the crowd stood awestruck. Joe had officially lost his job as bouncer to the young Ketchel, and he also lost Goldie's affection. As she was thanking Ketchel for helping her, Sid Lamont, a 19-year-old lightweight boxer with a good record, approached Ketchel and invited him to visit the gymnasium where he trained. When Ketchel arrived at Lamont's gym a few days later, Lamont invited him to spar, telling Ketchel that he wanted him to box with all the energy and moves that he could muster. Soon after the match began, Lamont felt the fury of Ketchel's aggressive style, calling a halt to the match and telling Ketchel, "You're built to order for this game, because you're a natural fighter with a wallop; the sort that don't need to be pretty to win. The ring's your meat kid, and you ought to go out and grab yourself some real coin."

After receiving Lamont's encouragement, Ketchel decided that boxing was his best option for securing the fortune that had been dreamt about since leaving home. He was thrilled and bewildered by the rapid turn of events. What would his mother and father think? Just a few years ago, he had wanted to be a cowboy, but now he was onto something real. In addition to Lamont, an old time fighter who worked in the mines had watched Ketchel demolish Joe and the three miners at The Copper Queen. When he found out that Ketchel was training at Reilly's gymnasium, he showed up and invited Ketchel to spar. The two put on gloves and the veteran knocked Ketchel around for a while. Day after day, they continued to spar, with Ketchel showing improvement each time. In a matter of weeks, Ketchel could almost fight the man to a draw.

"It got so every time we met, in the ring or out, we would go at it in a real brawl. He was a fighter of the gorilla style, and after two or three minutes, we would find ourselves rolling out in the middle of the street, with him on top of me trying to bite my ear off," Ketchel recounted.

In a matter of weeks, Ketchel's big break in the professional boxing ring would take place against the welterweight boxer, Kid Tracy, in a honky-tonk establishment in Butte. Seating boxes lined the establishment's second level, and the floor section contained a bar and tables. Tracy was essentially a show act, taking to the ring nightly to face amateur challengers. If he failed to knock his challenger out within four rounds, the prize money went to the challenger, even if Tracy had gotten the best of him. In the month preceding his match with Ketchel, Tracy put down all of his opponents with relative ease, but he had an unfair advantage. The honky-tonk's owner, Joe Halliday, knew that Tracy's loosing a match would be bad for business. Therefore, whenever Tracy faced a fighter that seemed to be giving him a challenge, he would hug his opponent and push him toward a curtain at the back of the ring. Behind the curtain, Halliday waited with a sandbag. When he saw the bulge of the challenger's head against the curtain, he would hit the unsuspecting fighter with the sandbag, either knocking him unconscious or dizzying him to the point that Tracy was assured a victory. Fortunately for Ketchel, Lamont had warned him about Halliday's dirty tricks.

At the sound of the opening bell on Sunday, May 3, 1903, the crowd watched in amazement as Ketchel sprang from his corner and punched Tracy across the stage. Tracy recovered by landing a quick jab. But a split second later, Tracy buckled at the knees as Ketchel countered with a right hook. Halliday ducked behind the curtain and Tracy promptly moved to Ketchel's right and began forcing toward the back of the stage. As they neared the curtain, Ketchel broke Tracy's hold and ripped a left hook that snapped Tracy's head toward the curtain. The curtain bulged and Halliday sent the sandbag crashing down on the skull of Tracy instead of Ketchel. Tracy fell to the canvas face first, and the rowdy audience cheered like never before. Lamont was the only person present who knew that Tracy and Halliday had been beaten at their own game, and he was one in a group of Ketchel's friends who had come to insure that Ketchel was treated fairly when he collected the ten-dollar prize from Halliday. Without them, Ketchel could have been beaten to death to eliminate Tracy's competition.

Despite the fact that Ketchel still growing and had yet to perfect his technique, his win over Tracy made him brag as if he were a champion, which ended up angering the celebrated welterweight, Maurice La Fontise, who soon challenged Ketchel to a fight. La Fontise's challenge would culminate in an epic battle that became a Butte legend, especially for how Ketchel, the amateur, went after La Fontise without the slightest sense of fear; and for how he sprang to his feet each time La Fontise put him on the mat. Ketchel ended up defeating La Fontise in the 24th round and, in the process, went from being a bouncer to a sought after and well-paid boxer. After defeating La Fontise, he went on to meet five of the best boxers in the neighborhood, knocking each of them out cold. Having earned what seemed like a fortune, Ketchel became the best-dressed man in Butte, sporting hand made cowboy boots, impeccably tailored shirts, silk neckerchiefs and the widest and whitest of Stetson hats.

Maurice Thompson, one of Ketchel's friends and boxing opponents from his bouncer days, had grown up to be a talented welterweight. He had always figured that he and Ketchel would meet in a professional fight someday, and not long after Ketchel's rise to fame, his hunch proved true. Ketchel wanted be in great condition for the fight. But he knew little about training and didn't yet have a trainer of his own.

Afraid of being ridiculed for his inexperience, he didn't consult other fighters, and devised an amateur training regimen that consisted mainly of running until he almost fainted from exhaustion. On some of his early morning jogs, Ketchel ran as many as 25 miles. Then, in the early afternoon, he would train for a few hours at a gymnasium, shadow boxing or sparring with anyone who would put on gloves. Ketchel thought that he was getting himself into great condition. But he was actually wearing himself down.

Ketchel would have wasted most of his stamina if his former boss, Josh Allen, hadn't dropped by to visit him at the gym. Although Allen had never boxed, he was a student of the game, and he realized that Ketchel was wasting precious vitality. Ketchel listened carefully to Allen's advice, and much to his amazement, discovered that Allen would be providing him with a boxing trainer whose services were paid in full. The trainer was Dan McQueen, a veteran middleweight who had fought both bare knuckled and with gloves. Under McQueen's guidance, Ketchel went through a consummate training routine that brought him into to perfect form.

The first fight between Ketchel and Thompson took place in Billy Nolan's clubhouse; an old building that had seats built around the ring in the style of a traveling circus. As Ketchel and Thompson advanced to the center of the ring and shook hands, Ketchel whispered to Thompson, "Listen, kid. Shall I go easy?" Maurice shook his head and replied, "Nothing doing, you fight your fight and I'll fight mine. I'm going to trim you. But no hard feelings, see?" When the bell rang, Ketchel rushed out of his corner, ducked under Thompson's left jab and drove him against the ropes, hammering his stomach with both fists. Thompson clinched and broke, and then a great crash attracted his and Ketchel's attention. The seats on the right side of the arena had collapsed, sprawling hundreds of patrons across the floor. Thompson stepped back, laughed and waved a glove toward the struggling patrons as they clutched at each other to regain their feet. Then, as Ketchel turned his head to observe the scene at greater length, something hit the back of his neck with such force that he instantly plunged to the canvas. Thompson had ducked behind him and unleashed a forceful, down-chopping right. By the time the referee reached the count of four, Ketchel hadn't moved. But a few counts later, Ketchel was back on his feet, albeit dizzily.

When the referee called action, Thompson stepped in and hit Ketchel with straight right to the jaw that sent him back to the canvas. Ketchel stayed on the floor for seven seconds, got up and dove into a clinch. After the referee broke them apart, Ketchel would go down three more times before the end of the round. But when the ending bell rang, he was on his feet.

Ketchel and Thompson slugged it out through the second round with the advantage going to Ketchel. He bloodied Thompson's eye and Thompson bloodied Ketchel's nose. Ketchel also landed two murderous rights—one to the body and one to the head—but generally had a hard time reaching Thompson. He still had much to learn about ring technique, and through the third and fourth rounds, Thompson obviously out boxed him. Ketchel had never recovered from Thompson's first round rabbit punch—a blow delivered to the base of the skull that can easily paralyze a fighter.

Nevertheless, Ketchel's great conditioning and aggressive style kept him battling at a furious pace, and by the end of the match, he was meeting Thompson punch for punch. Even so, it was too late to overcome Thompson's incredible point accrual from the first round. When the referee announced Thompson the winner by decision, Ketchel nodded in approval. Ketchel's first important fight in an important arena had ended in defeat. But it was the kind of defeat that earned the loser more notoriety than the victor. After 18 minutes of fierce brawling, Ketchel's unfettered style had made him Butte's biggest boxing idol.

"You're there, kid," Nolan told him later, "and you're good for a match at this club with any bozo of your weight. If Thompson is willing, I'll sign a return bout right off the reel. He'd never have beaten you if he hadn't chopped a sneak on you in that first round. You'll know better next time!"

Nothing would have suited Ketchel more than another go with Thompson. But Thompson was in no hurry to fight him again.

"He's made of pig iron," Thompson told Nolan. "I bounced him off that floor often enough to put a mule out of business, and he just kept coming back for more. What I need now is a rest. If you can't dig me up something a bit softer than I had tonight, I ain't interested for the present. Let some other mug have him."

Ketchel wouldn't fight Thompson again until October 21, 1904, when Thompson repeated in ten rounds. After their second bout was over, Thompson gripped Ketchel's hand and said, "That's enough Stanley. I've licked you twice, and I don't think any other man will ever be able to do it. I couldn't do it myself again. You're going to be world's champion some day."

The details of Ketchel's third match with Thompson are unclear, but Ketchel showed improvement from his second meeting with Thompson, and the ten-round fight was declared a draw. The Ketchel-Thompson series ended on December 29, 1904, with Ketchel and the majority of Butte feeling confident that Ketchel would become a champion despite his two defeats. In addition to the growing opinion of Ketchel's championship level talent, an event that would soon happen outside of the ring would make him more famous still.

Jack Stagel, owner of a large ranch near Billings, Montana, was one of Ketchel's admirers. On Stagel's invitation, Ketchel paid a visit to the ranch and made his childhood dream of becoming a cowboy a reality for a time. Despite appeals from Nolan and other boxing promoters to return to the ring, Ketchel spent several months with Stagel. It was his first real holiday. He rode horseback as he hunted on the open range, clad in the picturesque cowboy garb that he had dreamed of since childhood. Ketchel had always had a deep affection for horses and firearms, and he soon learned to ride and shoot as well as anyone on the ranch. But he was disappointed that the cowboy life didn't seem as alluring as it had in the western novels of his boyhood. There were no villains to reign in, or so he thought.

Soon after Ketchel arrived at the ranch, a man named Victor Ramon, who had murdered a Mrs. Wheatly, the wife of a Montana ranchman, was on the run. Ramon had also shot and wounded her husband, and injured their two small children in the process. The details of the murder have been lost to time, but it is known that Ramon successfully eluded the authorities for five days following Mrs. Wheatley's murder, during which time a dead or alive reward of $1,000 was placed on his head.

Late one night at the ranch, with the other ranchers having gone to town for entertainment, Stagel and Ketchel emerged from a stable after tending to a horse, when a rifle shot rang out in the darkness. A split second later, Stagel fell to the ground with a groan, grasping his shoulder. Ketchel ordered Stagel to stay down. Then he took his new six-shooter and fired back at the figure advancing out of the brush, Victor Ramon. The distance was too far for a revolver to shoot accurately, and Ketchel soon fell backwards against the ground, pretending as if he had been shot.

Ramon had come to the ranch in search of money and ammunition, and had hid in the brush until he saw the ranchers leave for Billings. After seeing Ketchel go down, he briskly stepped forward and approached Ketchel's motionless body. He nudged Ketchel with his boot to see if he would move, but he didn't. Then he brushed his boot against Ketchel's limp, open hand. Suddenly, Ketchel grabbed Ramon's ankle and jerked him off of his feet, causing his rifle to fly in air and land out of reach. As Ramon lay on his back, Ketchel leapt on top of him and ground his knee into Ramon's stomach. He cut off Ramon's scream by squeezing his throat, and then put the barrel of his pistol in Ramon's mouth. Ketchel relaxed for a second and then savagely smashed Ramon on the jaw, sending him unconscious. He dragged Ramon's limp body to the stables, bound his hands and feet with rope, and then went to check on Stagel. After staunching Stagel's wound, Ketchel and Stagel headed for Billings with Ramon in tow. Once at Billing's, Ketchel carried Ramon over his shoulder and dropped his limp body on the front step of the police station. Upon realizing Ramon's identity, the authorities quickly drug him into a cell.

After Ketchel received the one thousand dollar prize for Ramon's capture, he was treated to an even bigger celebration in Butte. A large vaudeville dance hall was rented for the occasion.

Chapter 5:
Ketchel vs. Tommy Ryan and California

Ketchel was back in action on July 7, 1904, when he knocked out Kid McGuire in a single round at Billy Nolan's clubhouse. 1904 was a busy year for Ketchel; he scored eleven knockouts, most of them coming within four rounds. The majority of his fights took place in Butte or Miles City. The following is a list of Ketchel's wins by knockout in 1904:

    Monday, June 20th – Jimmy Quinn MT KO 3
    Thursday, July 7th – Kid McGuire MT KO 1
    Friday, July 15th – Kid Leroy MT KO 1
    Sunday, July 17th – Young Giley MT KO 4
    Monday, September 5th – Bob Merrywell MT KO 3
    Thursday, September 15th – Jimmy Murray
    Saturday, October 15th – Bob Merrywell MT KO 3
    Saturday, October 29th – Jimmy Kelly MT KO 1
    Tuesday, November 8th – Kid Lee MT KO 8
    Thursday, November 10th – Joe Mudro MT KO 4
    Friday, December 16th – Jack Grimes MT KO 10

The next year, Ketchel continued to score a series of knockouts. The following is a list of his knockouts in 1905:

 Wednesday, January 14th – Kid Thomas MT KO 1
 Friday, January, 20th – Jack Bennett MT KO 5
 Saturday, March 25th – Sid Lafontise MT KO 24
 Thursday, May 18th – Sid Lafontise MT KO 7
 Sunday, June 4th – Curley Rue MT KO 11
 Tuesday, June 13th – Kid Pecor MT KO 5
 Friday, June 16th – Kid Lee MT KO 17
 Tuesday, July 4th – Young Kelly MT KO 8
 Saturday, July 15th – Bob Sennate MT KO 17
 Saturday, August 19th – Roy Hart MT KO 1
 Thursday, September 14th – Bob Sennate MT KO 11
 Friday, December 1st - Jerry McCarthy MT KO 12
 Saturday, December 2nd – Maryville Kid MT KO 3
 Friday, December 8th – Kid Herrick MT KO 7
 Friday, December 16th – Jack Bennett MT KO 5
 Tuesday, December 19th – Jerry McCarthy MT KO 11
 Sunday, December 24th - Kid Foley MT KO 4

Ketchel's name was huge in the state of Montana. But outside of Montana, his name was little recognized by boxing promoters. Later, they would later regret not pursuing Ketchel for fights, especially those who were familiar with his name. Nat Fleischer gave a good explanation about how slow sports news traveled in the early 20th century:

> Compared with today, sport news was not widely played up in the papers. There was no radio or television to broadcast the fame of local celebrities. Even the champion pugilists were accorded but a trifling amount of national publicity, and as for the smaller fistic "fry", few broke into print except in localities where they happened to have made ring appearances. Nowadays a fighter who accomplished one half of what Ketchel did in a two year period would

be ballyhooed all over the country. Picked up by some enterprising manager and billed in a star bout in one of the main boxing centers. But things moved at a slower pace then and when middleweight champion Tommy Ryan visited Butte with a show under Jack Curley's management, neither Ryan nor the promoter had ever heard of Stanley Ketchel. Tommy Ryan was one of the fastest most scientific prizefighters that ever donned a glove and he carried an effective knockout punch into the bargain, as his long and honorable ring record testified.

In 1904, Middleweight Champion of the World, Tommy Ryan, was traveling through the United States, meeting any challenger who was willing to fight him for four rounds. He was planning on retiring in the following year or so. But he was still an intelligent, adaptable fighter who remained at the top of the middleweight class. Ryan was knocked out only once during his professional career, when he arrived in horrible shape for a fight with Kid McCoy, who was supposed to take a beating. But Ryan would get revenge on McCoy the following year in 1897.

As he neared retirement, Ryan traveled the Vaudeville circuit and performed in numerous boxing exhibitions. Ryan's promoter, Jack Curley, tried to schedule Ryan against weaker opponents, but he soon made the mistake of soliciting Ketchel. When Ketchel agreed to box Ryan, his application was immediately accepted. Curley knew that Ryan's success on the Vaudeville circuit depended on one-sided smash fests, but he began to feel guilty that the boyish looking Ketchel would supposedly serve as Ryan's punching bag. The thought of Ketchel giving the champion a tough fight never entered Curley's mind. He could have never known that, since fighting Maurice Thompson, Ketchel's fighting style had become more fluid, his combinations more devastating and his defense much improved. Ketchel's favorite boxing strategy was cutting off the ring; a strategy in which a fighter makes the ring smaller by keeping his opponent from circling left or right. When Ketchel's opponents tried to circle, he would move in a straight line to cut them off, and then pin them against the ropes with a flurry of punches. But, while Ketchel was improving month by month, he still lacked the experience to put away a boxer as crafty as Ryan.

Compared to Ryan, Ketchel was still a novice in the finer points of boxing. But as they fought, Ketchel hammered away at Ryan with such vigor that Ryan began tiring from evading and blocking the assault. As Ketchel hollered and attacked Ryan, Ryan's speed and cleverness helped get him out of harm's way, especially in the last thirty seconds of the fourth round. But at the final bell, his face revealed a collection of small cuts, while Ketchel's was unblemished. At the end of the fight, Ketchel and Ryan shook hands, and neither Ketchel nor the audience accurately perceived the degree to which he had dominated Ryan, but Ryan did. Back in the dressing room, Ryan approached Curley with sarcasm.

"You're a fine manager," said the champion. "I suppose next time you'll go to the zoo and rent a Bengal tiger for me to play with. What in the hell made you pick that kid Ketchel?"

"Well hell," said Curley apologetically, "he was only a boy and he looked easy to me. He hasn't any major reputation and his name ain't in the record books. Why, nobody ever heard of him before!"

"Yeah," replied Ryan, "Well, I'm telling you something. They're going to hear plenty about that baby one of these days if he sticks to the punching racket. Why, blame it, I never put in a tougher four rounds in my entire life. Believe it or not, I had to scrap for all I was worth to keep from hitting the floor in that last round. You got to be more careful jack. I'm hoping to finish this tour all in one piece, not chopped up in sections!"

By the time Ketchel was 19-years-old, he had scored sixteen knockouts; by 1906, the Western United States was talking about how he had scored 32 knockouts in 36 contests. Sports writers from Chicago and San Francisco bestowed Ketchel the famous moniker, The Michigan Assassin, which would prove increasingly apt as time went on. In 1906, Ketchel ran up another list of impressive knockouts:

Monday, February 12th – Montana Sullivan MT D 20
Monday, March 19th – Warren Zubrick MT KO 2
Friday, May 11th – Paddy Hall MT KO 1
Friday, May 18th – Mike Tierney MT KO 7
Saturday, June 16th – Kid Lee MT KO 17
Wednesday, August 29th – Kid Frederick MT KO 7
Monday, September 10th – Kid Foley MT KO 11

The matches were fought in Montana Saloons. Not until the early spring of 1907 would Ketchel have the opportunity to box in unfamiliar territory. California newsman and journalist, R.A. Smith, of the *San Francisco Bulletin*, had watched Ketchel fight in one of the Butte saloons, and had afterwards introduced himself to Ketchel and recommended that Ketchel seek better fortune elsewhere.

"Get the hell out of this rat hole and you'll be coming back to Montana Society with a fortune and with glory," Smith explained. "You're too damn good a fighter to be wasting your time around here. Take my tip and go to the coast. You won't regret it. I know the fight game. I've seen the best of 'em. They don't come any better than you kid, and you'll never get anywhere hanging around the sticks. Look, here's a letter to a chap who runs a club in Sacramento. He'll be glad to see you and once you arrive in California it would be easy sledding for you. Take my advice kid. Do as I say."

Ketchel agreed and shook Smith's hand, thanking him. The next morning, he headed for the west coast on a freight train. Ketchel had more than enough money to pay for a ride, but his hobo instinct made drew him to hop a freight car and ride for free. It was beautiful weather when Ketchel arrived in California. He had made good time and reached his destiny looking a tad unkempt and dirty, but felt as though he could whip any prizefighter in the world. His confidence would soon be tested.

A clever, hard hitting African-American middleweight named George Brown made Sacramento his home. He was a big drawing card, had defeated some of the best middleweight contenders, and it wouldn't be long until he had his shot at the middleweight title. But first he had to beat Joe "Wonder Man" Thomas, whom he had fought to a ten-round draw in their first meeting in 1905; and before he meet Thomas on the 4th of July, he would have to beat Ketchel.

Both Brown and the promoters of his main event with Thomas figured that Ketchel would be easy work for Brown. The "hobo fighter", as Brown called Ketchel, figured to be cakewalk victory during the build up to his fight with The Wonder Man. Brown entered his match with Ketchel with a record of forty-two wins, one defeat and one draw, with thirty-three wins coming by knockout. During his training sessions leading up to the fight, Ketchel had impressed the sports journalists and boxing promoters as being as being stylistically crude and unorthodox. Little could they imagine what was to come.

A huge crowd of Marysville boxing fans was in Sacramento to see Brown fight Ketchel, and at the sound of the opening bell, Brown boxed cleverly and started off the fight in control. He continued his winning form in round two, playing a game of cat and mouse with the frustrated Ketchel. The match was going as expected, and the crowd anticipated the moment when Brown would tear into Ketchel and send him reeling. But when Brown stopped dancing and tried to come at Ketchel with power, Ketchel hit him with a terrific right hand uppercut to the chin, putting him on the canvas. Ketchel danced back to his corner while the referee went through the formality of counting Brown out. He could have counted to 1,000 had it been necessary. Ketchel's knockout blow had lifted Brown completely off of his feet. The crowd exited the building disappointed that Brown wouldn't be fighting a rematch with Thomas anytime soon.

The next day, Ketchel departed Sacramento for Redding via the rods of a Pullman car, leaving the fans as mystified about his identity as they had been when he arrived. Before Ketchel departed, the Sacramento club owner looked dismal as he paid Ketchel $500 for his fight with Brown. Inglis hinted to Ketchel that he might be interested in representing him instead of Brown, although he was anything but happy with Ketchel. Inglis had bet heavily on Brown, and there before him stood the reason why he lost. The next afternoon, a crowd of disappointed sportsmen gathered at the railroad station in Marysville to welcome home the fans who had attended the fight in Sacramento the night before. For weeks, organizations in Marysville had been planning a giant Pioneer Day celebration to be held on the 4th of July, intending for the main attraction be Brown versus Thomas.

Expected to become middleweight champion after Tommy Ryan's retirement, Joe Thomas had signed a contract that required him to meet any opponent that his promoters selected in a twenty-round bout on Pioneer Day. Thomas needed money. He had run out of "big time" opponents among welterweights and middleweights, becoming the only world champion in history who was forced to seek out weaker, more amateur opponents to make money.

Lou Trevor, appointed by the celebration committee to take charge of the boxing match, had made a diligent effort to match a nationally known fighter against Thomas. But his efforts had failed. He had wired flattering offers to Hugo Kelly, Jack and Mike Sullivan and "Honey" Mellody. But they wanted none of Thomas' superior ring cleverness and boxing skill. Failing in his efforts to secure big name competition, Trevor had been obliged to do the next best thing: pit Thomas against the rising George Brown. But he was forced to make yet another concession after Ketchel knocked out Brown.

"Who is this dirty hobo who knocked out Brown last night?" Trevor asked several Marysville sportsmen loitering around the depot. But nobody seemed to know.

Bill Barton, less affectionately known as the "Marysville Mauler", was a private detective employed by the railroad company. He was stationed in Marysville to arrest anyone who abused railroad policy or destroyed railroad property. Standing over six-foot-three and having an affinity for violence, he had established a reputation as the toughest "yard bull" between Sacramento and Portland, which had effectively made him the most despised man in Marysville. On numerous occasions, the townspeople watched in horror as Barton beat helpless hobos senseless with his blackjack. On the day of Ketchel's arrival, Barton was mingling with the crowd at the depot as he kept watch for a young hobo that the special agent's office in Sacramento had warned him was riding beneath the cars of the Portland limited. When the train rumbled into town after nightfall, Barton stood on the platform holding his blackjack, crouching to look under each coach as it slowly passed.

"Come here, you filthy bastard!" he suddenly shouted at the top of his lungs as the train pulled to a halt. He raced up to the side of the freight car, reached under it and grasped the coat collar of a smallish looking youth; it was Stanley Ketchel. Using all his strength, Barton gave a powerful jerk, loosening Ketchel's hold on the rods. Another powerful jerk and he had Ketchel standing upright beside him. Barton was taken aback that Ketchel didn't seemed frightened, and instead stood looking him straight in the eyes, grinning. When he observed that the crowd was laughing at him and not Ketchel, Barton's anger boiled over.

"Here's what hobo's get in town, you bastard," Barton shouted as he dealt Ketchel a terrific blackjack blow across the face. Ketchel's knees buckled, and for a moment it looked as though he was going down. Then, just as suddenly, he recuperated, assuming a fighting stance and pummeling Barton in the face with a flurry of punches. Pandemonium broke out at the depot. "Fight! Fight! Fight!" everyone seemed to be yelling in unison, rooting for Ketchel as he continued to get the best of Barton. The crowd soon swelled to thrice its original size and shouted joyously every time Ketchel landed a telling punch, and every time Barton swung his blackjack and missed. Putting everything that he had into one desperate punch, Ketchel landed a clean, bone crushing left hook to Barton's jaw, knocking him unconscious.

The crowd gathered around Ketchel and fought for a chance to shake his hand.

"Stay right in this town for the rest of your life and whip that punk every day," someone shouted, laughing hysterically.

In dramatic mockery, Barton was carried to a little park at the end of the depot and laid out with his hands folded across his chest, his bloody face placed directly under a faucet spout. The crowd kicked him on the soles of his shoes, a move that they had seen him perform on sleeping hobos. Then they ran water in his face to revive him. The boxing fans that had returned to Marysville on the same train quickly identified the winner of the brawl as Stanley Ketchel, the upstart boxer who had knocked out speedy George Brown in Sacramento the night before. During the excitement, the train had pulled out of town and, having nothing to do, Ketchel accepted the crowd's invitation to "stick around and help us celebrate the event we have been waiting for the last six months."

Ketchel was wined and dined all over town for the remainder of the night. In every café, saloon and dance hall, the sound of clinking champagne glasses could be heard as men and women drank, danced and sang to the health of "Kid Ketchel from Montana." Once again, Stanley Ketchel was a hero.

Chapter 6

Thomas vs. Ketchel I

The next day, Lou Trevor called a meeting with the other celebration committee members.

"You know, gentlemen, it may be just as well that George Brown got trimmed and fell down on us because this hobo from god-knows-where whaled him," Trevor said. "He sure is a fighting fool, a real sluggin' devil if I ever saw one. Of course, I think Thomas will waste him. As a matter of fact, I don't think nobody can beat Thomas around the welterweight and middleweight neighborhood. But I think that this brash youngster will give him a hot tussle while he lasts and he'll go down fighting. That's the sort of thing the crowd likes. Thanks to that big jackass, Bill Barton," he added, "there is not a man in California who would draw half the crowd in this town right now, that fellow will."

"Well, sir, I'd thought he'd have been around to see you soon as he arrived in town," responded Trevor's co-assistant and matchmaker, Cal Somers.

"No, haven't seen him. The boys have got him in tow, making

a huge fuss over him licking Barton. He's somewhere down the line having a good time. I want you to find him, Cal, and tell him I want to see him right away," said Trevor.

"Don't worry, I'll find him. He can't be too hard to find," responded Somers.

"One more thing," Trevor added. "If you don't find him, we'll have to dig up this fighter nicknamed The Michigan Assassin. The papers have been raving about this scrapper from Montana for quite some time. He's a big drawing card there."

"What if, sir, this kid we're searching for is the "Assassin?" asked Somers.

"Well Cal," Trevor said quietly, "I think we'll have a huge, mega fight in our hands, a bigger fight then we expected. Go get him."

Both men smiled, and then Somers left the conference room, closing the door behind him. Little did he know that they were hunting down a fighter who would become one of the great middleweight champions.

Somers found Ketchel later that night in Marysville's biggest dance hall. Ketchel, as light-footed as a cat, had Marysville's prettiest Vaudeville dancers for his partners. He spent a portion of the money obtained in his win over Brown to buy on of the finest cowboy suits that Somers had ever seen. Somers could hardly believe that, moving smoothly to the lilting ragtime tunes was the same young hobo who had knocked out the feared Barton. As soon as the music drew to a close, Somers introduced himself to Ketchel.

"Hello, my name is Cal Somers. A friend of mine by the name of Lou Trevor wants to see you at once. He's figuring on having you meet Joe Thomas for twenty rounds on the Fourth. Joe is heading for the middleweight crown and a lot of the wise newspaper guys recognize him as the champion right now. It's an opportunity of a lifetime for you, kid.

But you'll have to cut out this monkeyshine, night prowling crap and get into damn good shape. This here Thomas is a killer!"

Stanley chuckled and shrugged his shoulders. "Listen pal, I can't bother with Trevor tonight. I've got beautiful women to attend to and I've got a hot date. And anyway, I'm going to see this dance out to the finish. But you can tell him it's alright by me. I'll fight Thomas or any other man he wants to choose. They all look alike to me. Tell Trevor I'll meet him in the morning."

Somers was annoyed by Ketchel's lack of respect, but the memory of Barton being pounded to pieces on the station platform warned him that it might be well to keep his disgust discreet. Without further argument, he returned to meet to tell Trevor the news.

The following day, Ketchel met with Trevor and heard him explain the details of the match with Thomas. He learned that his end would be $1,000, win, lose or draw, with Thomas getting a guaranteed $2,500.

"Listen boy, I'm doing this to protect you," Trevor assured him, "so you won't be broke when the scrap is over. Joe Thomas is a tough hombre."

"So am I," retorted Ketchel. "You don't need to worry about me. I'd just as soon fight this punk winner take all, and you tell him so too."

"How old are you?" Trevor asked.

"Nineteen. Old enough to know I can whip any guy near my weight in the world. If you want to make easy money, have a bet on me. This Thomas bird ain't any tougher than plenty of other bimbos I've sent to the cleaners. A champion's only a wonder until some fellow comes along and belts him down. Watch me do some fancy belting on the Fourth."

"Well, son," replied Trevor, "the 4th of July is your chance to back it up. Also, I'd like some information about a scrapper from Montana.

The papers have been raving about him for some time now. They call him, The Michigan Assassin. Have you heard of him?"

Ketchel laughed and said, "He's standing right in front of you."

Trevor and Cal were instantly excited that Ketchel was the talked about "Assassin".

"I had a feeling you were the Assassin," responded Trevor. "Just making sure. Alright kid, the fight is on. You're going to fight Joe Thomas twenty rounds out at the ballpark on the Fourth, and you'll have to get into condition." Both men shook hands and the deal was settled.

On the morning of the 4th, Thomas and Ketchel weighed in at 160 and 147 pounds, respectively. But Thomas's weight advantage wouldn't play a factor.

At the sound of the opening bell, Ketchel rushed from his corner as if determined to end the fight with a single punch. Thomas stayed calm, defended himself well, and responded with strategically placed punches. However, Thomas soon realized that Ketchel's initial onslaught was not just a burst of energy; it was the way that Ketchel would fight from start to finish. In the middle of the first round, Ketchel delivered a powerful, straight right to Thomas's mid-section that sent him careening against the ropes. From that point forward, the crowd focused on Ketchel and cheered at every punch he landed.

Thomas held his own until the sixth round, when he began tiring from Ketchel's hits. But at the beginning of the seventh round, Thomas attempted to turn the tide by rushing from his corner and landing a series of aggressive rights and lefts. Ketchel was being fed his own medicine and had a hard time defending. But Ketchel began the eighth round with a vengeance and kept Thomas continually on the move, not allowing him to set up for his offensive sequences. Ketchel kept up his frenetic pace into the eleventh round, pounding Thomas' face and body in a manner that would have knocked out lesser fighters. In an effort to break up Ketchel's attack, Thomas threw jab punches, but to little effect. Then he wrapped Ketchel in a clinch in a desperate attempt to stop the action. Then, as Ketchel pulled out of the clinch, he delivered a pounding left hook to Thomas's jaw that sent him to the canvas for a nine count. Thomas had gone down near the ropes, and when got to his feet, he was still dizzy enough that he needed to hold the ropes for support. He spent the remainder of the round trying to avoid being knocked out, and he succeeded. Even when Ketchel hit him with powerful overhand right, Thomas managed to stay upright.

In the fourteenth round, Thomas was again in distress at the hands of Ketchel's frenetic style. But Ketchel was gradually tiring himself out; while Thomas's defensive posturing had allowed him to gather strength. Ketchel kept his lead going into the final round, but Thomas would soon tap his renewed strength and give Ketchel all that he could handle. The final round progressed and ended with Ketchel and Thomas trying desperately but unsuccessfully to knock each other out. It was a display of pure offense and the crowd cheered themselves hoarse.

After 20 brutal rounds, the fight was declared a draw by referee Ed Smith. In the aftermath, neither fans nor boxing critics could believe that Joe Thomas—a defensive wizard and deadly two-handed fighter—struggled against a young, inexperienced fighter. Yet, Thomas was still California's main boxing attraction and everyone felt that he would be the next middleweight champ.

When Bill Roche—a famous referee who was working as a matchmaker for James W. Coffroth's boxing arena—picked up the next morning's paper. He was amazed as he read of how the virtually unknown Ketchel had fought to a draw with Thomas. Suspecting that Thomas had been "robbed", Roche immediately realized the commercial value of a rematch between the two. Roche sent Ketchel and Thomas each a telegram, asking them to meet with him to discuss a rematch. Soon after receiving the telegram, Ketchel drove his red roadster to Colma, a small town just south of the San Francisco border, to Roche's immaculate office.

"Hello boys! I'm glad you could make it," began roach as Ketchel and Thomas entered his office. "I'm sorry I didn't see your scrap in Marysville, but I heard it was a thriller. I believe that a rematch will be better. I'll give you guys 50 percent of the house for a fight over the 45-round route. How about it?"

"Suits me," responded Ketchel, with Thomas nodding in agreement. Ketchel's calm indifference as to what arrangements were made astonished Roche. He was used to hearing fighters argue over every detail. After Ketchel gave his approval, he said very little, leaving Roche and Thomas to do the talking. Roche ultimately decided that the purse should be split 75 and 25 percent between Thomas and Ketchel, respectively. The battle was scheduled for 3 p.m. on Labor Day, and Thomas suggested that they fight at 160 pounds. Ketchel accepted the terms without qualm. The fight was set to happen.

Each fighter had put down $250 as a weight forfeit payment, and after weighing in on Labor Day and receiving his money back, Ketchel drove to a poolroom and bet the $250 on himself at odds of 1 to 2. After placing his bet, Ketchel drove back to the arena and looked for James Coffroth to ask him what he thought the gate receipts would be. Coffroth said he expected them to be no less than $15,000.

"Sounds great to me," said an excited Ketchel. "How about paying me over the loser's end right now as you figure it should be? I want to take my chances."

It was the first time in Coffroth's career as a promoter that he had heard such a proposition. Ketchel's confidence both impressed and astonished him. After Coffroth advanced him the money, Ketchel jumped back into his roadster, raced back to the poolroom and wagered every dollar that he would destroy Thomas. After Ketchel returned to the arena, Roche remonstrated Ketchel for not keeping some of the money just in case things didn't turn out the way he expected, which made Ketchel laugh.

"Let me tell you something, Billy, it's all or nothing with me," Ketchel replied. "I never hedged in my life for marbles or money. Don't worry about me. I'm due to win for sure. There's no fighter around my weight I can't pound to pieces inside of 45 rounds!"

Chapter 7:
Thomas vs. Ketchel II

"After knocking out about a dozen lesser lights, I was matched to meet Joe Thomas, who was a rising star on the west coast. We fought a twenty round draw at Marysville on July 4th, 1907. Thomas knew more about the game then I did at the time and was extremely clever in avoiding punishment. I felt, however, like another go with Thomas, and on September 2nd of the same year, we faced each other again in Frisco. It was a long and hard battle of thirty-two rounds, the longest fight I ever had." **Stanley Ketchel, 1909**

On September 2, 1907, Ketchel was preparing to fight Thomas for the second time at Coffroth's Mission Street Arena. The boxing events of that day began with the skillful black fighter, Kyle Whitney, nearly knocking out Ed Carter in front of a half full Mission Street Arena. Given the celebrative spirit of Labor Day, Coffroth figured that he wouldn't have a problem drawing a full crowd for the main event, and he was right. By the time that Ketchel and Thomas entered the ring, there wasn't an empty seat in the arena, and for the next two hours, the crowd remained on their feet.

The battle began with Ketchel running out of his corner, hooking a solid left to Thomas' body, and then missing with a straight right. Ketchel kept swinging and hooking, coming in close and delivering flurries of punches to Thomas's body. Thomas would set himself and shoot clean punches to Ketchel's head and body, but Ketchel remained unfazed. Despite the frenetic action, it wasn't until the ninth round that a knock down took place. Ketchel connected with a stunning hook to the left side of Thomas's head. It missed Thomas's jaw and landed square on his cheekbone, sending him to the mat. Thomas was barely hurt, but he decided to take a nine count to clear his head. With Thomas back on his feet, the fight continued with Ketchel crowding Thomas and Thomas pumping in his left jab upon charging Ketchel.

By the twenty-fifth round, the fight was even. Ketchel's aggressiveness was counter balanced by Thomas' cleverness, and vice versa. Each fighter landed hard hits and landed them often, and each of them was frequently staggered and stunned, but they refused to hit the canvas. As the bell sounded to open the 29th round, Ketchel made a mad dash to meet Thomas coming out of his corner. But Thomas was prepared for the rush and planted a solid right to Ketchel's chin, finally sending him to the canvas. The end of the fight seemed immanent. When the referee counted seven, Ketchel was on one knee and Thomas looked ready for the kill. But Ketchel suddenly rose and went on the attack, catching Thomas off guard and dashing his confidence. Near the end of the fight, Thomas was out boxing Ketchel by a significant margin. But Ketchel spent round 32 throwing punches from all angles and leaving Thomas guessing about the best plan of defense. Suddenly, Ketchel pounded Thomas in the stomach with a left, doubling him over. Then he hit him with haymaker to the jaw and sent Thomas careening toward the ropes, where he ended up hanging suspended. He was knocked out cold. Seeing his condition, Thomas's seconds mercifully tossed a sponge in the ring and saved him from further punishment. While Thomas's seconds were giving him smelling salts, the crowd went wild as Ketchel's hand was raised in victory.

Roche was astonished by Ketchel's incredible performance. Later in 1907, he would describe his ironic impression of Ketchel and his memories of Ketchel's second match with Thomas:

> The first time I ever saw Ketchel; he looked more like a clean-cut student than a husky prizefighter. But when he stepped between the ropes he became a different person. I was completely amazed by the transformation. He looked wild like an animal, and his body looked like it had been chiseled out of granite. From the first round he dug those terrific hooks into Thomas' guts and I, who has been hanging around fighters all my life, had to look away every time I heard that hallow thud of his fist sinking into Joe's middle. Thomas, a brave kid and wonderful boxer, fought back gamely. But his jabs were as effective as a rowboat against a battleship. He's stick one out. Ketchel would stick out his mug and take it. Then he'd sneer and uncork a hook into Joe's belly. Although Thomas wasn't cut externally he was throwing up blood from the fifth round on. I had a feeling that Ketchel was carrying Thomas, that he didn't want to knock him out because he was having too much fun tearing him apart. Then something very strange happened, or at least it was strange to me. Thomas somehow figured out how to step away from Ketchel's dynamite and at the same time counter with stinging rights to the chin. Inwardly, I egged him on. I hate to admit it, but I found myself doing things now and then, which favored Joe. As Ketchel came steam-rolling out of his corner for the 29th round, Thomas set himself and put every drop of strength left in his body behind a right to the chin. It landed with a booming thud

and there was Ketchel flat on his back. I didn't give him a chance to get up, but he fooled me, and everyone there. At seven he was on one knee clutching at the ropes. Just as I was about to call "ten", he was up. I was so astonished. It was Joe's last hope of victory. In the thirty-second round Ketchel slugged him with a left to the stomach and right to the jaw and it was over. I went to Jimmy Coffroth in the rear of the arena and told him there wasn't a middleweight or for that matter a heavyweight in the world who could lick this fighting demon Stanley Ketchel. There are some who insist that shorter fights of today are keyed to a faster pace. This one lasted thirty-two rounds and it appeared to me that any round was faster than any round I have seen in middleweight battle since. And I do not look back to the old one through rose-colored glasses either!

On his way back to his office, reporters surrounded Jim Coffroth. They wanted to see what he thought about the thrilling battle. Coffroth initially refused an interview. But when he opened his office door, he changed his mind. He turned around and said, "Never have I seen two men go at such a terrific clip over as long a distance, and never before or since have I seen a man able to hit as hard a blow as the two Ketchel landed after thirty-two rounds of cyclonic milling. Ketchel carried his punch longer than any middleweight ever breathed. He's the next middleweight champion of the world. There's no middleweight living who can beat Ketchel in a long bout of 45 rounds. This is all I have to say."

Manager Joe O'Conner described the scene in the dressing room between Ketchel and Thomas after the memorable battle: "After the fight, while both boys were in the dressing room, Joe Thomas was very much beat up. I heard him say 'I want Stanley'. I immediately told Stanley to go into his room. Both boys shook hands and tears came into their eyes. They never said a word."

Meanwhile, Ketchel was quoted in the *San Francisco Chronicle* as saying, "Well, I'm champion. I fought my way up from the bottom of the ladder, and I guess I showed those who were at ringside that I had some class. I'm in the business now, for a few years at least."

When Ketchel said he was champion, he was referring to the welterweight title, which Joe Thomas had claimed after defeating Honey Mellody. Ketchel's claim wasn't widely recognized, but there was no question that Thomas-Ketchel II was the talk of California. The historic battle marked the true beginning of Ketchel's career and boosted his fighting reputation to dizzy heights from coast to coast. Nevertheless, there were many Thomas fans that refused to be convinced that Thomas's star had faded. They pointed out that, for the greater part of the Colma battle, Thomas obviously had the upper hand, and insisted that, in a 20-round fight, Thomas would easily defeat Ketchel by decision.

Thomas's fans would get another chance to see Thomas fight Ketchel in a bout that would become a forgotten classic that some boxing historians feel was a better fight than Thomas and Ketchel's 32 rounder.

Chapter 8:
Thomas vs. Ketchel III

Upon being offered the opportunity to fight Thomas a third time, Ketchel immediately accepted.

"I have no animosity towards Joe," reported Ketchel. "But I am willing to pound him to pieces every night in the week if they ante up my dough for my trouble. But no hard feelings, Joe."

Thomas still felt that he could beat Ketchel in a shorter fight, and he knew that his third match with Ketchel would be his last chance for redemption. If Ketchel defeated him, Ketchel would take the number one spot in the middleweight division. Thomas's third try against Ketchel was scheduled for 20 rounds on December 12, 1907.

The 12th of December turned out to be a grim day. Ominous clouds billowed overhead and a raw wind howled, predicting cloud burst. By the time that Ketchel and Thomas were ready to begin the 10 p.m. boxing match, the thunderstorm that had started earlier in the day was at its height. The fight took place in the old professional ballpark in San Francisco's Mission District, where a huge circus tent had been erected to cover the ring and the ringside seats, with lower priced seats being covered by the grandstand.

The opening round was sensational. Ketchel continued his tactics from the previous match, delivering a left and then a right to Thomas's body, and then bringing over a hard right to the head. Thomas was practically lifted off his feet with a left hook to the jaw and then fell to the canvas. But he didn't stay down for long. He bounced to his feet and tried to stall out the round, dancing away from Ketchel's punches. Growing irritated, Ketchel pushed Thomas against the ropes landed a flurry of punches, one of which sent blood spilling from Thomas's nose. Thomas retaliated with a tremendous combination to Ketchel's jaw. Then Ketchel came back with a thunderous left hook, causing Thomas to buckle and fall into a clinch. Ketchel soon broke away and started landing punches to Thomas's body. In the last 10 seconds of the first round, Ketchel delivered a right hook to Thomas's chin that turned Thomas completely around. The spectators jumped to their feet as Thomas almost fell through the ropes at the sound of the bell.

In round two, Ketchel kept up his remarkable speed and continued to wear Thomas down. He missed with a powerful right and got one to the jaw in return. Then Thomas delivered a left to the chest, following it with a series of left jabs. Near the end of the round, Ketchel landed one of his deadly left hooks and broke Thomas's rib cage. Just as Ketchel landed the punch, the storm caused some of the overhead lights to burst, sending glass flying through the air. Ringsiders suffered cuts, and Ketchel and Thomas received small cuts on their chests and faces. But the fight's pace never slackened. Ketchel kept punching like crazy, while Thomas kept defending while slipping in jabs.

In round three, Ketchel punished Thomas so badly that even Thomas's defense was awkward and labored. At one point, Thomas started spewing blood over Ketchel's shoulder as they entered a clinch.

Ketchel tried over and over to land a clean right to Thomas's jaw but kept missing. Thomas did his best to measure his time and distance, trying to shoot his quick right to Ketchel's face. Ketchel landed terrific lefts and rights to Thomas's midsection that Thomas eventually countered with a stunning right to Ketchel's jaw. Then Ketchel tried to get in close and Thomas delivered a quick right to his ear, after which Ketchel hit him with a left and then a right uppercut to the jaw at close quarters. Still at close range, Ketchel shot a wicked left hook to Thomas's stomach, then Thomas shot a beautiful triple left hook to Ketchel's jaw. In the last 30 seconds of the round, Ketchel unloaded a flurry of punches that made Thomas cover up until the bell clanged.

Near the beginning of round four, Ketchel sliced Thomas's left eyelid open, causing blood to pour. Soon afterwards, Thomas landed a great right to Ketchel's chin. But Ketchel shook his head and rushed in for more. Ketchel forced Thomas around the ring and delivered a bone breaking right to the jaw. Thomas was staggered and clinched for dear life. As Ketchel broke out of the clinch, Thomas backed away in a hurry. But Ketchel was able to cut off the ring and trap him on the ropes, delivering incredible blows to the body that made Thomas double over. But to the audience's surprise, Thomas would come back with amazing speed and land a flurry of punches in return. Both fighters were maintaining a fast pace at the sound of the bell.

In round five, Ketchel used his left hook and jab effectively. Thomas tried several rights, but couldn't reach his target. Ketchel snapped Thomas' head back with a straight right to the mouth, further lacerating Thomas's already bleeding gums. Then he delivered a barrage of lefts and rights to Thomas's body. Thomas jabbed Ketchel's nose and it started bleeding. Then he ripped a right and left to Ketchel's jaw as Ketchel went for the body, the exchange ending in a clinch. With the clinch broken, Thomas shot a jab and missed a right cross as Ketchel sent pulverizing left hooks to his stomach. Ketchel jabbed Thomas in the face and slipped in a straight right, following it up with a combination to the body. Then he hit Thomas with a left hook to the head. Thomas countered with triple jabs to the chin. But Ketchel recovered and landed a right to Thomas's left eye, following it with an uppercut, a cross and a torrid left uppercut to the mid-section. Thomas jabbed at Ketchel's mouth and then threw a flurry of left and right uppercuts to the body. Then he hit Ketchel on the cheekbone with a straight right, following it with a series of left hooks. Ketchel roared back and landed a beautiful left hook that stunned Thomas, sending him wobbling toward the ropes. Ketchel rushed Thomas and almost bowled him out of the ring before the referee broke them apart. Thomas retreated but was hit with a right to the nose as he back peddled. As the round drew to a close, Thomas covered up while Ketchel punched like a madman.

At the opening of round six, Ketchel rushed out of his corner and met Thomas at center ring. Thomas looked heavy on his feet, but he quickly hit Ketchel in the mouth, jabbed him in the nose and hit him in the jaw with a right cross. Ketchel came back with rights and lefts to Thomas's head. Then, after exchanging body shots with Ketchel, Thomas landed a stiff right, which Ketchel countered with a thundering left and right combination to the stomach. Thomas ripped an underhand right to Ketchel's chest and then shot a wicked right to the body. After Ketchel delivered a right flush in return, Thomas jabbed two stinging lefts to Ketchel's chin. Ketchel tried to counter with a right jab but missed, and Thomas hit Ketchel with a hard left to the stomach. Ketchel and Thomas continued exchanging blows that did neither of them serious damage, when Ketchel suddenly belted Thomas with a powerful left hook to the mouth. Thomas was shaken and was trapped in his own corner. Ketchel tried to seize the opportunity and let loose a barrage of punches. But Thomas managed to evade every blow and hooked Ketchel in the head at the sound of the bell.

In round seven, Thomas started relying on his superior technical skills to counter Ketchel's tenacity. He landed a hard left hook to Ketchel's head, followed by a crisp right to the jaw. Ketchel came back with a left to the body that damaged Thomas' rib cage on the other side and then landed a solid right to the head. Thomas feinted and then spun and jabbed, sending two lefts to Ketchel's face. Ketchel's nose was busted wide open, and Thomas delivered three lightening quick rights to the face and a brilliant hook to the head. Ketchel worked to force Thomas to the ropes, throwing rights to the jaw, a left and a right to the midsection and a right to the chest. The last minute of the sixth round contained breath-taking action. Thomas blasted Ketchel with a left and a right to the chin and then delivered a wicked hook to the jaw. Ketchel slammed a crunching left to Thomas's head in return, but Thomas shot back with a left jab and right cross to the mouth. Ketchel finally tied up Thomas on the ropes. But the round was drawing to a close and Thomas scored with a nice jab at the bell.

The eighth round started off at a heated pace. Thomas looked like he was trying to take a page out Ketchel's book as he delivered a flurry of wild, hard punches. Thomas sent two stiff jabs to Ketchel's face. Then, after Ketchel missed with a swinging right, Thomas ripped a thunderous right to Ketchel's head. Ketchel was bleeding from above both eyes, Thomas had grotesque gashes beneath his eyes, and his nose was smashed almost flat. Ketchel put a left to Thomas's body and then Thomas jabbed and crossed Ketchel's chin. Ketchel pounded a left to Thomas's midsection and then landed an uppercut under the chin that snapped Thomas's head back. The spectators reacted to the punch with a groan as the staggered Thomas just as quickly ripped a left and right to Ketchel's body. Ketchel connected with a good jab and a straight right to Thomas's face, and Thomas was again shaken. Ketchel raced toward Thomas and went for the kill, slamming a marathon of hooks and uppercuts to Thomas's midsection. Amazingly, Thomas retaliated with a solid jab and a left hook to Ketchel's chin. After they exchanged explosive left hooks to the head, Ketchel pumped a left and a right to Thomas' splintered ribs. Thomas answered with short jabs to the head. Suddenly, Ketchel delivered a zipping left hook flush on Thomas's jaw that sent him careening toward the ropes. As Thomas desperately clutched the top rope to keep from falling into the press tables, the final bell sounded. The crowd gave a standing ovation as the heavy rain kept falling.

In round nine, a mysteriously rejuvenated Thomas astonished the crowd. On the brink of defeat at the end of round eight, he roared back to deliver his best round of the match. The ringsides marveled at his cleverness. As battered as he was, he was slipping, feinting and throwing punches in bunches. Ketchel missed most of his punches and got zinged by some great counter-punches to the head and body. Thomas was making Ketchel look like a novice and Ketchel knew it. Delivering graceful, clean blows with great hand speed, Thomas looked like he might put Ketchel away. But Ketchel never stepped backward and continued stalking Thomas, looking for the right opportunity. As Ketchel stubbornly stayed within punching range, Thomas hit him with a left jab to the chin and then delivered a left to the head. Ketchel responded by delivering a left to Thomas's liver. But Thomas came back with a flurry of jabs to Ketchel's face. Ketchel looked exhausted, but he managed to corner Thomas and land a sensational left hook at the jaw. How Thomas stayed on his feet was anyone's guess, but he quickly hit Ketchel with two rights to the face. Ketchel leaped through the air and hit Thomas with a right to the jaw. Thomas responded with a left and right combo to Ketchel's mouth. Then he hit Ketchel with a left hook to the head. Ketchel threw a right to Thomas's body and they continued to fight it out at close range. As in previous rounds, Thomas was punching Ketchel as the bell sounded, this time delivering a left hook to the jaw.

In round ten, Ketchel raced out of his corner and immediately landed a left and right combo to Thomas's stomach. Thomas made a good stand by landing a left hook to Ketchel's nose, following it with a solid right to the jaw. Then Thomas delivered a series of jabs to Ketchel's face as Ketchel went for Thomas's body. While Ketchel was still aiming for Thomas's body, he cleverly mixed in a crushing uppercut that caught Thomas under the chin. Thomas staggered around like a drunken man as Ketchel unleashed a swinging right to the jaw and another deadly uppercut that hit Thomas squarely in the face. Ketchel crowded Thomas and threw blows from all angles. But just when everyone thought the battle was almost over, Thomas exploded with a dynamic left hook to Ketchel's head. Ketchel was stunned and staggered backwards as Thomas proceeded to hit him with a right cross to the jaw. Then Thomas delivered two perfect hooks to the head. Just as Thomas had done, Ketchel managed to gather his wits and was exchanging blows with Thomas at the end of the round.

Round eleven picked up where round ten left off. Thomas stabbed at Ketchel's body and Ketchel hit Thomas in the midsection. Thomas countered with snappy left jabs followed by a right cross and then delivered hard lefts and rights to Ketchel's body. Then he hit Ketchel in the nose and made it bleed more profusely. After Ketchel blasted a barrage of punches to Thomas's body, Thomas threw flashy combinations to the body and head, connecting on some and missing on others. In the midst of the action, Thomas sent Ketchel to the canvas by shoving him. But Ketchel was on his feet in a split-second. The referee gave Thomas a warning and he fought cleanly for the rest of the round. Up from the canvas, Ketchel responded with fury and trapped Thomas in the corner. Hitting Thomas with two jabs and a hook, he then delivered a crushing right to the mouth. As the round ended, Thomas stayed covered up as Ketchel pounded away.

At the commencement of round 12, Ketchel exploded from his corner and bulled Thomas toward the ropes. Thomas doubled over in misery as the audience chanted for more carnage. Ketchel stabbed at Thomas's body and delivered a hard jab to the nose, and then he scored with a series of right crosses. Thomas was taking a savage beating as Ketchel sent a left to the side of his head in an attempt to knock him out. Thomas was now on the ropes with Ketchel pounding him in the stomach with right uppercuts. But he refused to fall and, as Ketchel pounded away, the bell finally sounded.

At the opening of round 13, Ketchel raced from his corner. But Thomas dodged to avoid the onslaught. Thomas's seconds had ordered him to circle and move instead of trying to match Ketchel's blows. Nonetheless, Ketchel managed to cut off the ring and trap Thomas in his own corner. Thomas quickly covered his face with his gloves as Ketchel tried to pound his way through them. With blood now running down his legs, Thomas seemed nearly gone as he clutched the top rope for support. Ketchel's attack on Thomas was so forceful that it caused Ketchel to break his wrist and dislocate his thumb. In less than a minute, he had unleashed a total of 55 punches, and every blow had found its target. Ketchel gave Thomas everything he had, and yet Thomas was still standing. Drained of stamina, Thomas sent a weak left to Ketchel's chin. Ketchel roared back, hammering Thomas's body and delivering a sharp left uppercut and a right roundhouse to the head. Then they clinched in the center ring and the referee intervened. Ketchel looked fatigued, but he kept delivering punch after punch. Hooks, crosses and uppercuts continued to pummel Thomas's face until the bell sounded.

In round 14, Ketchel rushed from his corner once more as Thomas slowly rose from his stool. As Thomas lumbered toward the center of the ring, Ketchel leaped in and whacked away with a left and a right to the body, then delivered a left hook to the chin. Once again, Ketchel had Thomas dancing on rubber legs, and he took advantage of it by bullying Thomas into a corner. As Thomas absorbed Ketchel's body shots, he summoned his energy and hit Ketchel with a right to the jaw, but Ketchel wasn't fazed. Thomas hit Ketchel with a right to the head and received right and left counters in return. After another of Ketchel's uppercuts was pounded into his mid-section, Thomas used his gloves to cover his stomach. While doubling over, he started coughing blood and was rescued by the bell. As he returned to his corner, his body began trembling and convulsing.

At the beginning of round 15, Ketchel burst out of his corner as usual and trapped Thomas in his own corner. Amazingly, Ketchel's macho style seemed to be getting stronger with each round. He delivered a slashing right that opened a ghastly cut on top of Thomas's head, and then proceeded to hit Thomas with a combination to the face, a combination to the body and a solid right to the jaw. Thomas was smothered by Ketchel's aggression and had little punching room. As he continued to take Ketchel's punches, he responded with a flurry of punches that was interrupted by a streak of lefts and rights from Ketchel. Ketchel delivered a torrid right and left uppercut to Thomas's midsection and Thomas doubled over, coughing up blood. Thomas tried to cover up, but Ketchel zipped a devastating one-two to the jaw. Finally, Thomas toppled to the canvas for a second time. The audience felt that Ketchel had pulled the fuse on Thomas, but Thomas was still game. He was on his feet at the count of nine. But the bell rang just as the action resumed.

After 15 rounds, Thomas was fighting on heart alone. His face looked like ground meat and his body was pocked with welts. Ketchel didn't look much better. Blood continued to stream from his nose and swollen lips, and large lumps protruded from his brows. Nearly the entire canvas was covered in blood. Even referee Sam Berger's sleeves and chest were smeared with crimson. Heavy rain poured into the ring and made the mat increasingly slippery. Thomas had little sand left in his hourglass, but he kept trying to fight back. As the round got started, Ketchel whipped a left hook to Thomas's mouth, a right to his jaw and a left to his cheekbone. As Thomas lay against the ropes absorbing Ketchel's onslaught, he suddenly seemed to come back to life. The roles were instantly reversed as Thomas exploded with a dozen lefts and rights to the head and body. Ketchel covered up and blocked most of the shots. But he was soon stunned by a series of bruising left hooks and brilliant right crosses and fell into a clinch. With the clinch broken up, Ketchel continued to defend and slip in straight-arm punches. As Thomas gradually wearied, Ketchel bounced back with a left and right to the body. Then Thomas ripped a devastating left hook to the jaw and followed it up with body shots. As the bell sounded, Ketchel was chasing after Thomas, trying to trap him in a corner as the crowd erupted.

After Ketchel steamrolled out of his corner to begin round 17, Thomas began using his jab. But after Ketchel hit him with a single right to the jaw, Thomas was back on the ropes. As Ketchel delivered a series of powerful punches to the head and body, once again, Thomas's strategy became survival. As Thomas did his best to defend, Ketchel suddenly switched to a southpaw stance, pulverizing Thomas with right hooks and straight lefts followed by a ripping right uppercut under to the body. As a natural lefty, Ketchel had trained himself to fight in both stances. After connecting with several punches southpaw style, Ketchel returned to the orthodox stance and unloaded a series of lefts and rights. Thomas was in distress as he continued to cover at the bell.

In round 18, Thomas emerged from his corner with both gloves shielding his face. Ketchel charged after him with flying fists. He whipped a right to Thomas's chin followed by a smashing left hook. After hitting Thomas twice in the head, Ketchel connected with a left and right to the body and then shot killer right and left swings to Thomas's jaw. Thomas was forced against the ropes once more. Thomas's head was spinning as Ketchel continued to pound away. As Thomas continued to cover up and hope that Ketchel's stamina would lessen, Ketchel again assumed a southpaw stance. He slugged a right and left to the body and pumped a quick left flush to Thomas's cheekbone. As Ketchel went for the body, Thomas covered his stomach in agony, which left him open upstairs. As Ketchel tried to connect on right jabs and solid lefts to the face, the fighters clinched at the bell.

At the beginning of round 19, Ketchel again raced from his corner and quickly forced Thomas into his corner. Ketchel had Thomas back on the chopping block and swung at Thomas's face with crosses, hooks and uppercuts. Thomas shuddered and spewed blood, but Ketchel didn't let up. He shot a wicked right hook to Thomas's ribs and connected on a mean hook to the teeth followed by a torrid right cross. Thomas was no longer replying with punches of his own. Ketchel rallied with beautiful uppercuts to the inside, popping Thomas' head back. Then Ketchel unleashed a whirlwind of rights and lefts to Thomas's body and head. Again, Ketchel turned Southpaw and delivered blinding right hooks and straight lefts to Thomas' chin. His next move, a ghastly right jab to the mouth followed by a right cross, prompted Thomas to clinch him. After the referee pulled them apart, Ketchel retuned to orthodox style and moved to center ring. Thomas staggered toward Ketchel and swung a looping left and right. Ketchel ducked the punches and delivered lead rights to Thomas's chin. Thomas' knees buckled and he slumped backwards. Ketchel pursued him and delivered a flurry of punches to the body as the bell sounded.

At the beginning of round 20, Thomas looked like he had been through a slaughterhouse. His face was beaten beyond recognition, with ghastly cuts and gashes consuming his face. His right eye was swelled shut and his left eye was barely open. Horrible welts protruded from his body, and his nose was so flattened that it was barely visible in profile. Thomas's broken bones had also hobbled him. In the end, he would suffer a smashed cheekbone, broken jaw, splintered ribs, broken hands and a row of loose upper teeth. But Ketchel was compromised as well; he had broken wrists, a dislocated thumb, a busted nose, massive swelling on his brows and a long cut across his lips. As the round opened, the fighters touched gloves and the bloodbath continued. Ketchel tore into Thomas's body with a tremendous flurry of hooks and uppercuts. He then bombed a head-cracking right cross to Thomas's jaw. Thomas became a noodle and staggered backward toward the ropes. Ketchel rushed him and ripped a sweeping right cross to the head. Thomas fell to the canvas and the crowd cheered, thinking that the fight was over. But as the referee began his count, Thomas amazingly stirred and struggled to his feet. He was furious that Ketchel had punched him as he was going down, and he looked ready to stand his ground.

Thomas would gather all of his remaining energy and go down fighting. As the fight resumed, ringsiders were enraptured by the intense fierceness of the exchange. Ketchel hammered Thomas's body and ripped right crosses to the jaw. But Thomas scored with lightening fast jabs and whipped a swift left hook, right cross, left hook combination to Ketchel's head. Ketchel shoved Thomas backwards but Thomas returned with stiff jabs along with another left hook to Ketchel's jaw. After Thomas's brief flurry, Ketchel parried a series of jabs and then delivered a straight right with his open glove. Thomas slugged three more hard jabs at Ketchel's nose. But Ketchel carefully evaded the shots and then delivered a straight right followed by right cross to Thomas's cheekbone. Thomas's head almost spun completely around and it looked as if his neck could have been broken. He was in serious trouble as Ketchel hurled a shower of lefts and rights to the body. Suddenly, Thomas dropped to the mat like a wet rag. The spectators, including Ketchel, were now supremely confident that the match was over. But they were wrong. Everyone stood in utter disbelief as Thomas returned to his feet. Thomas looked like a man coming back from the grave as he made it to his feet just in time. As he clutched the top rope to steady himself, the night air was filled with a symphony of screaming fans. As horizontal rain poured into the ring, thunder rumbled and lightening zigzagged across the sky, Ketchel and Thomas went at it again. Thomas swung a right and Ketchel ducked. Ketchel then delivered a left and right to Thomas' head followed by three lefts to the chin. He slugged a right into Thomas's body and then a left followed by two left hooks to the chin. After Ketchel missed with a right and parried a jab away from his face, Thomas feinted a right and then shocked Ketchel with a left hook to the mouth. Then he rammed Ketchel's body with two rights. As the fight bore on, Thomas was landing punches but Ketchel was landing more hurtful ones. Neither fighter gave an inch and there was no let up. But Thomas was soon wobbled by a left chop to his jaw. He looked knocked out on his feet and Ketchel tried to flatten him. But fate would be kind to Thomas as the bell saved him from taking more punishment. One of the most vicious middleweight fights in the annals of American boxing was finally over, and the referee raised Ketchel's right hand to declare him the winner.

The ring was so dark and the storm so loud that legendary ring announcer, Billy Jordan, had to climb into the blood soaked ring and shout at the top of his voice: "The winner by decision, the Michigan Assassin, Stanley Ketchel!"

The fans cheered as Ketchel was hoisted on top of O'Conner's shoulders so he could wave to the audience. Both fighters congratulated each another at ringside for a great fight. But Thomas's defeat signified the end of his reign as California's star fighter.

Thomas never fully recovered from the loss and the physical punishment he absorbed in his third battle with Ketchel. But the rival middleweights would face each other yet again after Ketchel had become a mega sports celebrity throughout the nation. It was his third victory over Thomas that made Ketchel the most feared middleweight of his time. Like Ketchel, Thomas had dreamed of becoming a world middleweight champion. But his dream would never become a reality. Stanley Ketchel was the better boxer.

Chapter 9:
Ketchel and the Sullivan Brothers

After Ketchel defeated Thomas for the third time, he was left with four worthy adversaries in the middleweight boxing world: Jack and Mike Sullivan, Billy Papke, Tony Caponi and Hugo Kelly. Ketchel would eventually fight all four, but the Sullivan brothers were first on his list. Twins, the Sullivan's were born on September 23rd, 1878, in Cambridge, Massachusetts. Multitalented, they had incredible tenor voices. But after discovering their boxing prowess, they made the ring their occupation. By early 1904, with their reputation well established in the east, they followed the advice of Horace Greeley and headed for California, where they continued their success and quickly became fan favorites.

On April 23, 1907, Mike fought the tough "Honey" Mellody, who had won the world welterweight title from Joe Walcott, the "Barbados Demon". In addition to the Sullivan brothers, Mellody was also a source of boxing pride for Massachusetts, making the fight an electric event. At the end of 20 rounds, Sullivan won by decision. As Mike's reputation grew on the heels of his victory over Mellody, Jack's reputation received a boost when he fought Hugo Kelly to a 20-round draw. However, being more popular than Kelley, boxing fans and critics alike bestowed Jack the victory in the court of public opinion.

In 1908, Mike, the lighter and faster of the twins, was set to fight Ketchel in a match that was important to each fighter as they pursued the middleweight crown. Ketchel was willing to fight either brother, but Jack had responded to Ketchel's initial challenge by telling Ketchel to fight Mike first, and that he would see him in the ring if Mike lost. The Sullivan's denigrated Ketchel for his hobo status and hurled other insults that appeared in the newspapers, angering Ketchel's admirers. But Ketchel sensed uneasiness behind the Sullivans' bravado and remained calm.

When a reporter asked his opinion of the Sullivans' comments, Ketchel replied: "Looking at the statement makes me laugh, it must be great to feel yourself so big that you can high hat any guy that gets in your way, but I never could make the grade as a four flusher. When I was a kid my mother used to read to me out of a book about the Civil War. It told about a chap who was such a patriot that he was willing to send all his relatives to the front to fight for his country, though he preferred to stay home himself and pray for victory. Probably Jack Sullivan figures things out that way."

That same day, Ketchel accepted Jack Gleason's offer to match him with Mike Sullivan and signed a contract for a 20-round fight that would to take place at Mission Street Arena on February 22, 1908.

Prior to the fight, Ketchel had planned on reuniting with his family in Grand Rapids after a nine-year absence. When Ketchel's mother received his letter saying that he was on his way back to Grand Rapids, she was taken aback that he had chosen boxing as his line of work. But her shock was soon overwhelmed by her joy for his return. Nine years before, he had told his mother that the family fortunes would change when he returned home, and he was right. Stanley's friend and manager Joe O' Conner would come along for the reunion that would take place on Valentines Day. On February 14, 1908, Ketchel talked about his upcoming battle with Sullivan and his emotional reunion with family in Grand Rapids in a letter that he wrote to the sports editor of the *Rocky Mountain News*:

> Well, old man, I am back from my visit to our old home in Grand Rapids and have to settle down to hard training. I expect to win with ease from Sullivan. But will take no chances by going into the fight out of condition. I understand Sullivan hasn't much of a wallop and no man can ever beat me who hasn't got that. No man has ever come anyway near putting me out and I was fighting middle and heavyweights when I was in Butte and weighed about 119 pounds. Can't see how any fancy boxer is going to be any danger to me in a bout of forty-five rounds. I understand that Lewis beat Sullivan in Denver when you were managing Lewis. I am going to carry the fight to him from the start and it isn't going to last any longer than I can help. We are to weigh at 160 pounds, four hours before the fight, and that will put me in the ring at my very best. After I beat Sullivan I am going to claim the middleweight championship and will be open to meet any man in the world at the limit of that class, 160 pounds ringside. If you stop to think about it, nobody has fought for the middleweight championship who had a right to do so, since Bob Fitzsimmons fought Jack Dempsey (The Nonpareil) at New Orleans years ago. I am feeling fine. Expected to stop over in Denver for a few days visit with you on my way back to California, but they sent me a ticket over another route and I had to go that way. I suppose some people will say that I am picking a lemon in Sullivan, because he was knocked out twice by Joe Gins, but I was willing to meet any of them and Sullivan was the only good man they could find of my weight who was willing to fight me. Papke and Kelly are the boys I want to fight, and

I am ready for either of them just as soon as my fight with Sullivan is over. I challenged the winner when they fought in Milwaukee and was in hopes one or the other would accept. Neither one seemed very anxious to do it, although they both knew that they could get more from one fight in 'Frisco than from a dozen of those bush fights like they are fighting right along. I don't say they were afraid and I never said they were dubs, as I was quoted as saying in some of the papers. They know their own business and if they don't want to fight me that is their business. Say, old man, I had a great time on my visit in Grand Rapids. It was a great reunion, I spent six weeks with the folks and it was the happiest six weeks in my life. My mother was so glad to see me that she cried all day, the day I came home and, though as I am, I did a bit of crying my self. Dick, I wouldn't go away from that dear old mother of mine for a single day if I could have her with me in my business. She worries about me getting hurt in the ring, but I made her think it was not near as bad as they tell about and she feels better now. I am going to settle down some of these days and she will be with me always. Father was tickled to death to see me, too but you know my old man don't say much. My brothers were so happy they didn't know what to do. My father is coming out to see my fights and is going over in Denver to see you. Just put a bet down on me to beat Sullivan in less than fifteen rounds and you will win. I see where Naughton had a nice story in the Examiner about you and was glad to see it. They all say you are the best posted writer on boxing in that part of the country and you are well known out here. The Rocky Mountain news must be a great paper, from what they say about it. With highest regards, I am your friend.

On the day of his fight with Mike Sullivan, Ketchel was heading toward his dressing room when he passed one of Sullivan's handlers, who carried a basket of oranges. Ketchel curiously asked what he wanted with such a supply of fruit.

"I'm taking them over to cut up for Mike," was the second's reply. "He likes to suck a piece of orange between rounds. There are two dozen here."

Ketchel laughed and said, "Tell Mike for me he's wasting his money. He won't need any oranges tonight."

As if fate had heard him speak, Ketchel's prediction would come true. The fight lasted less then one round, with a total of four punches delivered, all of them by Ketchel. Soon after the fight began, Ketchel delivered a crisp left hook to the jaw that put Sullivan on the mat. As the referee counted, Sullivan groggily assumed his feet and then attempted to circle away from Ketchel's attack as Ketchel hounded him. Within a few seconds, Ketchel managed to pass a bone breaking right through Sullivan's guard that sent Sullivan to the mat face first. As Sullivan returned to his feet once more, Ketchel immediately delivered a pounding right that broke Sullivan's jaw and sent him sprawling on the canvas yet again. As Sullivan fell, Ketchel delivered a haymaker to Sullivan's midsection that put him down for good. Just 78 seconds after the opening bell, Sullivan had been counted out, his head resting under the bottom rope. Nearby lay Sullivan's bottom teeth and a gold crown that had been knocked loose by Ketchel's right to the jaw.

Roche, with a horrified look, mumbled, "My goodness, he is dead."

Sullivan seemed to stop breathing, but with slapping and rubbing, he was finally revived after five minutes and carried back to his corner. With his brother still seeing stars, Jack Sullivan quickly challenged Ketchel: "You were damn lucky that wasn't me, a man of your own weight in there; and when we meet, things will be different. I'll lick you any day."

"Alright, if that's the way you want it, you're next," Ketchel replied.

Jack Sullivan did some serious thinking after his brother's fight. He now knew that Ketchel was more dangerous than had he thought, and he remembered that his own brother had ceased breathing after Ketchel knocked him out. However, in the name of brotherly honor, he had no intention of defaulting on his promise to fight Ketchel. After all, he had been in the ring since 1898, and his record included victories over some of the best contenders in the middleweight class. Thinking of his success, Jack gained confidence that he would end Ketchel's reign, and even thought well enough of his chances to bet $1,000 on himself.

Coffroth's Mission Street Arena was selected for Ketchel's fight with Jack Sullivan. The 35-round fight would take place on May 9, 1908, in the same ring that Ketchel had destroyed Jack's brother in. Jack, in his challenge to Ketchel, had said that Ketchel wouldn't punch him around like he had done to Mike, and he was right. Jack was a better fighter than Mike, and he had revenge on his mind. But Ketchel had a supreme motivator as well: the vacant Middleweight championship of the world. If he beat Jack Sullivan, he could finally say with confidence that he was middleweight champion.

As the fight neared commencement, Jack Sullivan entered the ring in front of thousands of his loyal, cheering fans. Then Ketchel entered the ring to the same reception. But the most important spectator for Ketchel was his father who sat ringside.

Sullivan wore a toupee that he had removed for his fight with Ketchel, making himself look a bit defeated before the fight even began. Compared to the 20-year-old, boyish looking Ketchel, the 35-year-old Sullivan without his toupee looked like an old man. But he was nonetheless in excellent fighting condition. Sullivan's supporters thought he would send Ketchel back to Montana in a casket, and for the first five rounds, it seemed as if their daydream had a chance of coming true. Sullivan began by beating Ketchel on points by relying on his technical skill. But by the eighth round, Ketchel's deadly power was showing heavily in his favor. And by the tenth round, it was all Ketchel. From then on, it was seemed obvious that, barring a miracle punch from Sullivan, Ketchel would knock him out.

Before the conclusion in the 20th round, Ketchel introduced his famous signature move that boxing fans called the "Ketchel Shift". Ketchel wouldn't put the shift into play until later rounds when his opponent was worn down. To execute the move, Ketchel would purposely misplace his right foot and miss with a right punch, only to pivot back from the intentional miss with an explosive left hook or a round house. When Ketchel used the shift on Jack Sullivan, he hit Sullivan the ribs with such force that it caused Sullivan to spew blood and fall into a heap. When Sullivan finally regained his feet after a nine count, Ketchel drove him against the ropes and clipped him in the chin. The hit to Sullivan's chin would have been enough. But as Sullivan fell, Ketchel delivered a crushing body blow just as he had done to Sullivan's brother. As the referee counted to ten, Ketchel could feel the burden of his longing for the middleweight title slowly lifting. Finally, he was champion of his division. Billy Jordan, stepped inside the ring to present Ketchel as champion to the roaring spectators: "Ladies and Gentleman, with a minute remaining in the 20th round, your winner by a 20th round knockout, the new world middleweight champion, the Michigan Assassin, Stanley Ketchel!"

The crowd gave both Ketchel and Sullivan a tremendous sendoff; and as they left the ring, Thomas Kiecal laughed with joy as he embraced his son and congratulated him on his triumph. Then Joe O' Conner leaped over the top rope and hugged Ketchel around his bloody, sweaty body. After navigating through the sea of reporters and fans, Ketchel immediately sent a wire to his mother and brothers back in Grand Rapids, telling them of his victory. The wire read: *I have won by Knockout in the 20th round your son and brother is middleweight champion of the world I'll see you soon.*

In response to Ketchel's victory, the *Grand Rapids Herald Newspaper* quoted Ketchel's mother as saying, "Am I happy? Of course I am. My boy is now a champion and a Idol to everyone across the country. He told me not to worry so I didn't. I always had faith in Stanley and always will."

Following the fight, a reporter entered Ketchel's dressing room and asked him what his mother's reaction would be when she heard the outcome. Ketchel smiled and said, "I think mother would be the happiest women in the world. I gave her my promise before I left Grand Rapids at 12 and at the reunion. That things It would be different when I see her again, I might have had to fight for dear life in this dangerous world on my own, but it was worth it and I accomplished one of my major goals and bring back home a fortune that my folks never thought they would see in their lives and I am going to purchase the most beautiful farmhouse they ever saw and plenty of land."

After securing the middleweight title, Ketchel became a darling of the sports world. Invited to countless fancy parties and befriended by the rich and famous, Ketchel's list of friends and acquaintances soon read like a high society guest list. But his most fortuitous relationship that resulted from his fame would be with his mother's childhood friend, Colonel R.P. Dickerson, a successful Missouri banker, businessman and sports buff. Dickerson had been a private in the Spanish American War. But in Springfield, Missouri, he was known as the "colonel." Dickerson's father, Jerome, had owned acres of woodland and became prominent in the Michigan timber business. His family had departed Grand Rapids and settled in Springfield by the time Dickerson was 20. With his father's backing, the younger Dickerson had opened R. P. Dickerson Mortgage Bank in Springfield, and soon grew it to a capital of $500,000. The colonel also owned a jewelry store and became the Ozarks' wealthiest millionaire, as well as a major player in the lumber business.

Having read about Ketchel's triumphs and emotional reunion with his family in the newspapers, Dickerson decided to attend Ketchel's championship match and afterwards joined O'Conner, Ketchel and Thomas Kiecal for dinner. Having bought his parents a new home in Michigan, at just 20 years old, Ketchel was already living a life of fame and fortune. But his association with Dickerson would provide a bridge for his success to reach greater heights still. But first, he would have to face another of his worthy middleweight adversaries, Billy Papke.

Manuel A. Mora

House of Stan's birth

STANLEY KETCHEL, W

Ketchel Attributes His Enormous Strength to
Pine Woods as a Lumberjack. Ketchel Ch
Training Work. The Accompanying Phot
Carrying a Log Back to His Training Quart

Manuel A. Mora

This is the church where Stanley Ketchel's Mass was held.
Copyright Manny Mora July 2001

Manuel A. Mora

Stanley Ketchel's gravestone.
Copyright Manny Mora July 2001

Stanley Ketchel attended St. Aldebert Parochial School
Copyright Manny Mora July 2001

Stanley Ketchel

Manuel A. Mora

Author, Manny Mora standing at Stanley Ketchel's gravesite monument.
Copyright Manuel Mora July, 2001

Manuel A. Mora

Stanley Ketchel

Manuel A. Mora

Stanley Ketchel

Manuel A. Mora

Stanley Ketchel

Manuel A. Mora

Stanley Ketchel

Goldie Smith   Walter Dipley

Chapter 10:
Papke, Kelley and, once again, Thomas

In the mid spring of 1908, Ketchel brought his family to a sprawling white farmhouse located on over 206 acres of property about nine miles north of Grand Rapids, in Belmont. It was their new home that he had paid for with his winnings. He also had built a private training camp on the property that, according to one Grand Rapids newspaper, was worth $28,000. Ketchel would visit the new house many times throughout the rest of his career. After an extended visit with his family to help them settle in, Ketchel headed back to California. He was not finished celebrating his victory over Jack "Twin" Sullivan.

Upon arriving in California, Ketchel and Joe O' Conner's son, Tommy, went on a wild spending spree that focused on wine, women and song. According to the elder O' Conner, Ketchel's taste for women and partying was uncontrollable:

> After Stanley came back from Michigan I gave him his money, amounting to over $3,000, a very foolish thing for

me to do as I soon found that all his friends were wearing $40 dollar suits. I immediately took the rest of the money and put it in the bank in his name. I then sent Stanley with my son up to Uklah, a beautiful town in California. Arranging for them to get whatever they wanted and charge the same to me. In two weeks time I called up to see how the boys were getting along, was presented with an itemized bill. I called those boys into the office and asked them how they spent over $ 300 in two weeks in the country. In glancing over the bills I found they were charged with horses four or five times on the same day. I called Stanley to my office, after asking what the charges mean. He turned around to my son and said, 'You take some of the blame too, Tom.' I called Tom in, Tom hung his head and scraped his foot and said, 'It was girls Pa.' I immediately sent them away from that town, where there were no young girls and no horses. A town 26 miles from Healdsburg sent them five pounds of candy, a gun and a Kodak camera and they were contented. I then matched Ketchel with Billy Papke.

Ketchel's claim to the middleweight title was now universally recognized. But his two outstanding rivals, Billy Papke, of Illinois, and Hugo Kelly, of Chicago, were eager for a chance at the crown, and Papke would get his chance first. Papke was born William Herman Papke on September 17, 1886, in Spring Valley, Illinois, and eventually moved west to Kewanee. After briefly working as a miner, Papke, like Ketchel, decided that boxing would be his way of making a fortune. His professional debut was in November 1905, and resulted in a six round draw with the clever Battling Hurley. Tom E. Jones was Papke's manager throughout his career, and he felt that Billy would be middleweight champion someday. In over two and a half years of fighting, Papke had not suffered a single loss. Though not facing top competition, Papke had earned a significant reputation due the cruel manner in which he took to knocking out his competitors. His unceasingly frenetic style had earned him two nicknames: the "Kewanee battler" and the "Illinois Thunderbolt". Billy's signature move was called the "Loop the Loop", in which he would work his opponents against the ropes, lay his head on their chest and then place his left arm under their right arm. Instantly, the opponent would take firm hold of the arm, after which Billy would turn toward his left, bringing his right hand up and around from the outside to land constant punches dead on the face with frightful force.

In 1907, Tommy Ryan finally vacated the middleweight crown that he held for over a decade and, by the end of the year, only four men were viewed as being obstacles to Papke's becoming the new champ: Jack Sullivan, Hugo Kelly, Tony Caponi and Ketchel. After Ketchel had eliminated Jack Sullivan, Papke eliminated Hugo Kelly by defeating him by decision after fighting him to a controversial draw in their previous match. Papke fans billed his second affair with Kelly as a championship decider. When Papke won, they called him the middleweight titleholder and wanted to see him beat Ketchel decisively. Some people remained unconvinced that Ketchel was a marvelous middleweight, preferring to view him as a trashy hobo from the sticks who didn't deserve to be the champ. Papke, they thought, was the optimal choice to take Ketchel's title away.

For his fight with Ketchel, Papke wore his trademark jockstrap with a cup protector into the ring without any trunks, leaving his buttocks exposed. As the rules didn't prevent it and it offered the greatest freedom of movement, it wasn't uncommon for prizefighters in the early 20th century to wear only a jockstrap. Ketchel, on the other hand, preferred to wear bright red trunks. Despite his humble attire, Papke was extremely cocky and let it be known that he considered Ketchel an overrated nobody. But he would soon find out otherwise.

As the bell opened the first round, the action got instantly under way. Ketchel quickly opened with a left hook that caught Papke flush on the jaw, sending him to the canvas with a thud. Papke was down for the first time in his career, and the shock of the situation was evident on his face. Stunned but not hurt, Papke was up in an instant and began backing away from Ketchel's attack. Throughout the rest of the round, Ketchel played for the body as Papke did little more than jab and sidestep. Papke was embarrassed that he was sent to the deck in the first four seconds of the first round and came out with fire in his eyes at the start of round two. He rushed out at the clang of the bell and ripped two hard rights to Ketchel's head. But Ketchel cleverly countered with deadly rights to the face. The pace was furious as they battled around the ring, and Papke, due to a hurricane finish that had Ketchel against the ropes when the bell sounded, obviously won the round.

The third and fourth rounds were similar to rounds one and two. Repeatedly, Ketchel met Papke's rushes with right and left uppercuts. But Papke shook his head and waded in for more. They were both bleeding profusely from the nose and mouth as the fourth round came to a close, and Papke's right eye was almost swollen shut. Despite Ketchel's relentless attack, Papke didn't give any ground in the fifth round. But he occasionally tried to clinch to avoid Ketchel's terrific body blows. Toward the end of the round, Papke drove Ketchel to one knee when he caught him with a magnificent straight right to the jaw, scoring a knockdown.

In round six, Ketchel was unable to connect with as many blows as Papke, but his punches were more powerful. He met Papke's repeated rushes with straight lefts to the mouth until Papke's lips looked like smashed grapes. Eventually, Ketchel landed a smashing right to the jaw that sent Papke to the canvas for a second time. Papke landed on his knees and got up at the count of eight. Then, as soon as the action resumed, Ketchel delivered a left haymaker that almost sent Papke flying through the ropes. A hard right hand to the stomach doubled Papke over in agony, and Ketchel was measuring him up for the knockout when the bell sounded. At the start of round seven, Ketchel leapt from his corner and immediately ripped hard rights and lefts that caught Papke on the chin. Papke responded with stabbing jabs to the face. But Ketchel took them with a grin and continued his vicious attack. Soon, he had Papke on the ropes and delivered a flurry of combinations to the body. The bell found Papke in a desperate clinch.

Round eight was the most brutal of the match, with Ketchel chasing Papke around the ring and receiving dozens of light jabs to each of his solid hits. They stood toe to toe and swapped blows for the remaining two minutes of the round, and the ninth round found them just as active. They faced each other head on, both landing hard rights to the face a few seconds after the bell opened the round. Ketchel then delivered an uppercut and followed it with a right to the jaw and a dozen more uppercuts. But Papke stood his ground and landed several hard blows as well. One of the punches stunned Ketchel. But when Papke came rushing in for what he thought was the kill, Ketchel instantly revived and they were mixing it up as before when the round ended.

At the opening of round ten, Ketchel swung a hard left that missed and then ripped a hard right to Papke's chin after breaking from a short clinch. Then he cut off the ring and forced Papke against the ropes, landing a right and a left and then missing with the same combination. Ketchel then delivered a right to the stomach. Papke fought back furiously and landed a left to Ketchel's mouth, breaking away from the ropes. Then Ketchel engaged Papke in clinch and forced him back toward the ropes. With Papke on the ropes, Ketchel successfully pulled off his "shift", leaving Papke wobbling and holding on to the top rope. Papke managed to recover, but for the last 30 seconds of the round, he merely circled Ketchel as Ketchel tried to knock him out. With the fight over, Ketchel was awarded a unanimous decision over Papke, handing him his first loss. Referee Jack McGuin raised Ketchel's hand and the arena celebrated. Ketchel was without question the king of the middleweight division. After the fight, Papke was still confident that he could beat Ketchel and pleaded for another go with the champion in a longer match.

"Ketchel certainly is a wonder," said a bitter Papke, "but I think I can beat him over the longest route. I was not at the least distressed at the end of ten rounds, and could have gone any number of rounds without trouble. Ketchel didn't daze me at anytime, whereas I think I was in trouble in the eighth. I don't want to distract from Ketchel's credit, but just give me another chance at him. I have already challenged him."

Ketchel readily agreed to a rematch, but Joe O' Conner had other plans for him. He was already working on negotiations with Jimmy Coffroth to match Ketchel with Hugo Kelly, Tony Caponi or Heavyweight Champion, Tommy Burns. When it was announced that Ketchel would fight Hugo Kelly at the San Francisco baseball club, tickets sold out in less than a week. But to the disappointment of the spectators, Kelly didn't have much to offer.

In 1908, Dean of American Sports Authorities, Bill Naughton, summed up Ketchel's July 31, 1908, 20-round fight with Kelly as follows:

> The battle between Hugo Kelly and Stanley Ketchel was finished with a solid left hook on Kelly's unprotected jaw before the final round had gone twenty – five seconds. Ketchel snuffed out the championship aspirations of the Chicago Middleweight. It was a blow that came as unexpectedly to the 10,000 people as it did to the man who ten seconds later was defeated. The Italian, was extremely confident in the beginning of the fight. He opened the round with a left jab

into Ketchel's face. As he left himself unguarded, Ketchel took advantage of the situation, for shifting slightly. Stan hooked his left and it landed flush on Hugo's jaw. Dropping face first to the floor, where his head struck with a crash, Kelly lay helpless for several seconds, then tried desperately to rise to his feet as referee Jack Welch kept up the ten count. The effort was way too much for one who had received such a shocking blow and Kelly face first fell back to the canvas and mad no further attempt to move as Welch counted him out. It was no accidental punch that Ketchel put over, he knew that he had a hard opponent in front of him, that Kelly's judgment of distance and the body punches that Hugo was landing as his rival was coming in, might be dangerous. Ketchel was always the aggressor, and was ready for the last punch once the opportunity was afforded him. The kayo blow came with incredible speed and it went true to the mark with terrific force. The champion did not emerge unscathed from the battle. Though an enormous lump was raised over Kelly's right eye in the opening round, the Italian sent home many wicked lefts and rights that brought blood to Ketchel's mouth. Powerful body shots added to the discomfort of the titleholder but through it all, Ketchel kept coming in regardless of the punishment he was getting and continued fighting like the devil. Ketchel was the best sensational fighter the middleweight division had produced since "Nonpareil" Jack Dempsey was in his prime. Not even the future heavyweight Champion Jack Dempsey could compare with the youth from Grand Rapids in point of color and mean tiger - like aggressiveness and relentless attack mixed with fantastic hitting power. "Way to many people underestimate Stanley Ketchel before they enter the ring with him. Let me tell you that soft-spoken kid is a fighting demon, with tons of heart and courage that helps him get through his grueling fights. There is only one Stanley Ketchel and there will probably never be another like him and that's saying a lot. He is the king of real life melodrama, unequalled as a dispenser of shock surprises in the world of pugilism. Not yet 21 and still a boy, Ketchel is already a national sports icon and has the whole country looking forward to his upcoming battles.

With Papke and Kelly under his belt, Ketchel was scheduled to face another middleweight threat in Tony Caponi. There were rumors that Ketchel was going to fight Caponi in Grand Rapids, and that Ketchel quickly had agreed to battle the Italian without O'Conner's permission. O'Conner's overprotective nature was wearing on Ketchel. More and more, Ketchel was doing as he pleased: racing cars, pursuing women and generally enjoying himself. O'Connor, like R.P. Dickerson, regarded Ketchel as a son and tried to protect him from the pitfalls of sports stardom. In the end, he convinced Ketchel not fight Caponi in Grand Rapids. In late 1908, he gave the reason for his decision:

> I feel as though I owe some explanation to the admirers of the game in coming here and refusing Stanley Ketchel permission to box in his hometown. I have various reasons. I feel as though I can't take chances considering the fact that I had trouble bringing him where he is now, the champion middleweight of the world. In the first place, Stanley is no fancy Dan boxer, and the moment he puts his foot in the ring there is something doing, and I understand, it is unlawful here to allow fights. The fight could only be stopped in the first round and the people would get nothing for there money. Stanley agreed without my permission to box Caponi, which means nothing to him, financially or otherwise, while Caponi has everything to gain and nothing to lose. I have no guarantee that he would box and feeling that there is so much at stake, I do not wish to take any chances on the matter.

With Ketchel's fight with Caponi canceled, O'Connor put him up against a man that he thought that he was finished with a long time ago:

Joe Thomas. After a strong discussion with O'Connor, Ketchel bitterly agreed to fight Thomas once again. Longing for the bigger payday that would have come with Caponi, Ketchel felt he wouldn't gain anything by whipping Thomas a fourth time. But O' Conner had completed the deal with Jim Coffroth, and there was no turning back. The fight would take place on August 18, 1908, in Colma, with Eddie Smith refereeing. Although over 12,000 spectators gathered to watch the fight, by that time, Thomas was regarded as a has-been. Weighing in at a soft 180 pounds, Thomas looked like a fat heavyweight. Ketchel, on the other hand, entered the ring with a ripped physique.

Most of the first round passed uneventfully. But as it drew to a close, Ketchel landed a fearful right to Thomas's body. Then, just as quickly, Ketchel employed his "shift" and planted a hard left over Thomas's eye. Thomas slinked to the canvas. But he quickly resumed his feet, and managed to last out the round without falling again. At the opening of round two, Ketchel missed on a couple of lefts. But he soon connected with a left hook to Thomas's body, after which they entered a clinch. After jabbing Thomas with a left, Ketchel missed on a forceful headshot and they clinched once again. During the clinch, Ketchel belted Thomas's body with his left, and when they separated, Ketchel connected with left to Thomas's body and followed it with a left hook to the jaw. Thomas connected with some left jabs, sending Ketchel back a few of times. But the punches didn't pack much power. As they came together for another clinch, Ketchel led with his right and then shot a hard left to Thomas's stomach. As Thomas doubled up and dropped his defense, Ketchel delivered a left hook that pummeled Thomas in the eye, sending him to the mat in a heap. With arena shouting for more, Thomas slowly regained his feet, standing tall but unsteadily at the count of seven. As the action resumed, Ketchel punched from all angles, looking for the decisive blow. But the round was far advanced and the bell spared Thomas.

Both of Thomas's eyes were swollen shut. But he wanted to go on and his seconds didn't discourage him. When Thomas staggered across the ring at the start of round three, Ketchel quickly delivered a right that missed. After entering a loose clinch, Ketchel whipped an awful right to Thomas's stomach. After rushing him to the ropes and hammering away at Thomas's midsection, Ketchel forced him toward the center of the ring. A couple of lefts to Thomas's jaw were followed by a cracking uppercut that sent him flying through the ropes, unconscious. After being helped back into the ring, Thomas lay lifelessly on his back, and the veteran timekeeper, George Harding, began the ten count. Thomas didn't twitch and Ketchel was declared victor, the crowd roaring in adulation as Thomas's handlers carried him to his corner. When he fought Thomas for the fourth time, Ketchel was at his best, while Thomas was at his worst. It was the last time that Ketchel would fight Thomas, and it was also the last time that he would fight under Joe O'Conner.

By the summer of 1908, Ketchel's relationship with O'Conner was getting rocky. Ketchel felt that O'Conner was holding him back from bigger paydays, and that O'Conner's protective nature was better suited to an up and comer than a champion like himself. However, Ketchel's acceptance of the divisive Willus Britt as his new manager—an arrangement that would see Britt collect 40 percent of Ketchel's winnings—would prove that the young Ketchel needed protection from fame's perils. Prior to Ketchel, Britt's meal ticket had been his brother, James Britt, a highly touted lightweight fighter. Yet, even family evoked no decency in Willus, as he claimed a whopping half of his brother's earnings. According to legend, when Packy McFarland knocked James down during a bout, Willus shrieked from James's corner, "Get up, you bastard, have you no regard for my feelings?" James prudently stayed down, and it resulted in the worst set back for Willus since 1906, when the city of San Francisco refused to pay him for the damage done to some of his real estate by the great earthquake. The city said the quake was an act of God, to which Willus pointed out that churches had been destroyed. The city conceded the point, but still declined to pay.

However, if Willus Britt was a proverbial devil, Joe O'Conner was a kind of puritan when it came to Ketchel. As the dates of Ketchel's bouts drew near, O' Conner would sometimes lock him in a boarding house, taking away all of his clothing, except his undergarments. Amazingly, it was in just this situation that Britt persuaded Ketchel to do away with O'Conner's harsh ways. With Ketchel locked in a boarding house, Britt ascended the building's rain pipe and entered Ketchel's room through a window.

"Let him lock you in, Mr. Ketchel…He can't keep me out, and you and I have very important business to discuss."

"Who are you?" Ketchel replied.

"I, sir, am Willus Britt, and, I might add, your new manager."

"Yeah? What makes you think so," retorted Ketchel.

"Listen kid, that joker you have now don't know anything," said Britt. "Stick with me and we'll be reeking with greater wealth and have a good time. Where are your clothes?"

"My manager's got them," Ketchel replied. "He always takes my clothes when he goes out and he locks me in so guys like you can't talk me into quitting him."

"Think nothing of it," said Britt. "Let's go to Jim Coffroth's saloon. He's got spare pants."

In 15 minutes, Britt had convinced Ketchel that he would reach greater heights if he accepted Britt as his manager. With Ketchel believing in Britt's predictions, the new team climbed down the rain pipe and set out for Jim Coffroth's. O'Conner's precise reaction to Ketchel's defection has never been clear. But it is known that he wasn't surprised that Ketchel succumbed to Britt's lures, and that he feared Ketchel would burn out from pursuing nightlife under Britt's permissiveness. Some of Ketchel's biggest fights would occur under Britt's management. But one of the most legendary events in Ketchel's career would result from him acting as his own manager.

Chapter 11:
Ketchel Knocks Out Four Heavyweights in one Night

A week after Ketchel had defeated Thomas for the last time and accepted Britt as his new manager, he traveled east while Britt remained in San Francisco, trying to line up big paydays. Ketchel hadn't been in New York for more than three days when Britt sent a wire ordering him back to California at once. Ketchel was slightly miffed; he had some big social plans in New York. But business came first, so he bought a ticket for the next train headed west. When he arrived in Denver, he decided to take short respite to break the monotony of the trip. After checking into a downtown hotel, he lit a cigar and strolled out to the street where a large red and blue prize-fighting poster caught his eye. The sign advertised a heavy weight boxing tournament in Leadville. When he found out that Leadville wasn't far from Denver, he raced back to the railroad station and bought a ticket to the small town. Boxing in an amateur, one-night tournament sounded like fun. But there was a problem: it was a heavy weight tournament and Ketchel had the appearance of a wiry youngster. When the train pulled into Leadville, Ketchel headed for the nearest shoemaker and had an extra pair of heels nailed into his shoes to increase his height. Then he visited a mining supply store and purchased two chunks of solid lead, each weighing about ten pounds, and placed then in his hip pockets. Still, Ketchel would have a terrible time convincing the tournament's promoter that he was strong enough to fight men who were older and stronger.

"Go home kid, before you get hurt," the promoter advised him.

But Ketchel kept arguing his legitimacy and finally the promoter surrendered: "All right you dumb kid, go on and get your brains splattered around the ring, maybe it'll teach you a lesson."

When asked for his name, Ketchel gave Willus Britt's name in place of his own, and then the fun started. In his first match, Ketchel, who looked completely out of place alongside the murderous, 200-pound brawlers from the mines, drew a bearded brute that worked for the Kearney Mining Company. Ketchel knew that he could easily get hurt and would have to use his entire hitting force if he wanted to win.

For the first minute or so of his first match, Ketchel danced around the ring, sizing up his opponent. Then he delivered what he thought was an ordinary left hook to the miner's chin. To his complete surprise, the big man fell backward, his head landing on the canvas with a thud. The promoter, who watched hopefully from ringside, looked up in complete amazement. He was praying that Ketchel wouldn't get killed, and Ketchel ended up knocking out an amateur heavyweight with one punch. But Ketchel's night wasn't over. He had to fight a second time and his opponent would be tougher.

Soon into his second fight, both Ketchel and his opponent were covered in each other's blood, and Ketchel's left eye was swollen shut. As always, Ketchel was delivering his punches as if he fired them from a machine gun, and his opponent's jaw and ribs were feeling the pain. Whenever Ketchel landed a solid punch, the heavyweight would pick him up and try to slam him to the canvas, pleasing the raucous crowd. After receiving a final warning, the miner would box fairly, which gave Ketchel the obvious advantage. In the fourth round, Ketchel sent his 230-pound opponent to the mat with a deadly left hook, leaving the crowd stunned. The tournament's next night was its last. After knocking out two more opponents, Ketchel would face the tournament's second survivor in the grand finale.

Ketchel was having the time of his life. He was the middleweight champion of the world and was fighting before an audience that had no idea about his identity. Ketchel had become the fan favorite of the tournament, and he obliged his new admirers by knocking out his final opponent in another bloody battle. Soon after the match, Ketchel collected his $40 purse and started to leave. But the promoter grabbed him by the arm.

"Damn, kid, stick around for a while, you're a big hit. I'll give you $60 a fight. How about it?"

Ketchel looked him in the eye and laughed happily. "Sixty bucks is a lot of money," he said gleefully. "But I'll have to turn down your offer. Thanks anyway."

Once back in Denver, Ketchel sent a wire to Willus Britt. It read: Just had four fights, won all four, made forty dollars. Here's fifteen bucks your share.

With Ketchel headed west, Jimmy Coffroth and Willus Britt were settling negotiations with the Papke camp and soon agreed that Ketchel and Papke would face off on Labor Day in Los Angeles. Under Britt's management, Ketchel wasn't preparing for his battle with Papke with much effort, wooing women and racing his roadster instead of heading to the gym. The rematch between the Michigan Assassin and the

Thunderbolt was most anticipated match of 1908. But while Ketchel was having a good time, Papke was training hard. Both fighters bubbled with confidence, with Ketchel claiming he would stop Papke inside of fifteen rounds, and Papke scoffing at Ketchel's bravado.

"This is a three to one chance," Papke said. "I am right and believe me when I say I will stop Ketchel before the fight has gone the limit."

Papke was so confident that he placed at least $3,000 on the line. He stuck faithfully to his training regimen, usually starting the day with stretches and then a brisk run, which he followed with an hour of swimming and two hours in the gym. Papke avoided the nightlife and chose to rest. But he continued to taunt Ketchel in the newspapers.

"They can call him the assassin and all the names they please, but that doesn't make me afraid of him. All that talk about his knocking out his sparring partners is a joke. He does that for affect. Anybody can knock out sparring partners, so it doesn't look to me that Ketch is any demon. Its time for America to say goodbye to Stanley Ketchel and meet their new king," Papke proclaimed.

With over 15,000 spectators buying tickets, the Jim Jeffries Los Angeles Arena was sold out. On September 7, 1908, the sporting world would witness a shocker. According to the *San Francisco Chronicle*, the bout would end as "the bloodiest in ring history."

Chapter 12:
Ketchel vs. Papke II

As Ketchel and Papke neared their 3 p.m. fight time on Labor Day, the Jim Jeffries Los Angeles Arena's crowd was already at a half roar. Dotted with political, sports and film celebrities, the sea of faces looked down on the empty ring and waited for action. Ketchel entered the ring first, wearing his usual red trunks, with Willus Britt and handler Pete Stone climbing in after him. Then Billy Papke entered the ring, wearing his scant uniform of a strapped cup protector and no trunks. His manager entered close behind.

Papke walked to Ketchel's corner with a grin and shook hands with him, and then they posed for photographs. When the introductions were over, both fighters were called to the center of the ring for final instructions. The former heavyweight champion, James J. Jeffries, was the referee. In Ketchel's era, all boxers knew that a cheap shot could get a fighter instantly disqualified, so little instruction was necessary. It was also customary for fighters to tap gloves just after the opening bell of the first round. But Papke, a shrewd battler with a one-track boxing mind, was always out to win any way he could.

After the bell opened round one, Ketchel extended both gloves, expecting a tap from Papke. But Papke instead pummeled a straight right at Ketchel's neck, hitting him squarely in the Adam's apple, and following it up with another straight right that smashed Ketchel on the bridge of his nose. The combination instantly made breathing difficult for Ketchel and caused both of his eyes to swell shut. Carrying on, Papke led with a left and forced Ketchel into a corner, landing four blows to Ketchel's head. He then stepped in to go for the body, but Ketchel caught him with a left jab. Undaunted, Papke came back with a fast left followed by a hard right that dropped Ketchel to the canvas.

With the crowd stunned, Ketchel groggily arose to his feet and Papke looked set for the kill. As the action resumed, Papke delivered a fast left and right to Ketchel's jaw that sent him down yet again. This time Ketchel waited until the count of nine to take his feet. But as soon as he got up, Papke swarmed in with another series of punches to the face and Ketchel was flattened thrice. Drawing mostly on will power, Ketchel gained his feet just as the bell rang and ambled to his corner.

In round two, Ketchel was still groggy as he came out of his corner, and Papke came in like a tiger. One of his punches caught Ketchel in the face with such force that it sent Ketchel staggering across the ring. Ketchel's face was a mixture of blood and bruises, but he refused to bow out so early, and he would soon get some help from Papke himself. As had happened in times past, Papke was tiring from his torrid offensive pace, and Ketchel finished stronger than he started, landing several impressive punches before the close of the round.

In round three, Ketchel appeared to be picking up steam and was soon dictating the fight. He gave as much as he received and, what he gave was stronger than anything served up by Papke. By round four,

Papke was covered from hand to shoulder with Ketchel's blood, and he caught Ketchel in the mouth for the first punch of the round. With his eyes almost shut, Ketchel failed to connect with the hardest blow that he had thrown at Papke. But he managed to end the round respectably, making it seem as if Papke had yet to arrive at a clear advantage.

Ketchel's broken nose allowed him little oxygen, and he kept snorting out chunks of blood and spitting up blood between rounds. But by round five, Papke's frenetic pace combined with the few good punches that Ketchel had landed had rendered Papke almost as weak as Ketchel. Amazingly, Ketchel seemed to be winning the fight, and the referee had to pry him from Papke's clinches with regularity.

Papke opened round six with a solid right to Ketchel's jaw. Neither man had been knocked out before, but Ketchel looked well on his way to being carried out of the ring for the first time in his career. Just before the bell sounded, Papke landed a terrific left to the pit of the Ketchel's stomach and Ketchel appeared to be going down when the bell sounded. Amazingly, Ketchel got the better of Papke in round seven and had Papke in distress. Stiff lefts to the body and head had Papke looking to clinch until the sound of the bell.

In round eight, both fighters sparred cautiously. But Papke soon delivered a series of lefts to Ketchel's face that yielded a new, steady flow of blood. Papke's fans were clamoring for a knock out, and Papke stepped in with a flurry of punches, landing several uppercuts to the inside that had Ketchel on the verge of collapse at the bell. With Ketchel's eyes swollen shut, Papke landed punches at will. The crowd stood and cheered as Papke sent another barrage of uppercuts to Ketchel's jaw. Both men were soaked in blood but still standing at the end of round nine.

In round ten, Ketchel clinched repeatedly and made it difficult for the referee to pry him from Papke. As Papke went to his corner at the round's conclusion, he waved to his cheering fans, while Ketchel sat in his corner suffering from a concussion and a severely broken nose. His fans were all but silent, sensing that his championship days were nearly finished. But at the opening of round eleven, Ketchel gave them a glimmer of hope as he rushed from his corner to meet Papke in the center of the ring. But the hope was short lived; Papke soon landed a left and right to Ketchel's face that made him spurt blood down Papke's back as they clinched. The crowd began yelling for the referee to halt the one-sided affair, but he turned a deaf ear. Papke would soon enough end the fight himself. He delivered a hard left hook that stunned Ketchel and then proceeded to land a series of blows that drove Ketchel through the ropes and into the laps of pressmen, who assisted him back into the ring as the bell sounded.

At the opening of round 12, Papke delivered a quick right that sent Ketchel to the canvas. As he regained his feet, Ketchel was a helpless, groggy figure that was immediately sent back to the mat by a straight right. As the count reached nine, Ketchel managed to gain his feet. But the referee immediately signaled to Ketchel's handlers to take charge and stop the fight. Britt knew it was the right thing to do and decided to throw in the towel. At 4 p.m., Jim Jeffries raised Papke's hand, signaling him as the new middleweight champion of the world. R.P. Dickerson, who was at ringside, sent a wire to the Ketchel's family a few hours later announcing the bad news.

Following Ketchel's defeat, The San Francisco Chronicle quoted many of Papke's dicey statements about Ketchel, most of them containing the following bravado: "I always knew I was the best man. I guess the public now will take some stock in my story in the Milwaukee fight. After that fight, I knew I was Ketchel's master and only wanted a return match to prove it. My fight has proved it. You noticed I didn't shake hands with him. The time we fought before he hit me when I shook hands with him and this time I took no chances. I got him first that is all."

This was Papke's greatest moment. He stunned an entire arena by beating a man who was presumed unbeatable. But Ketchel's shot at redemption would arrive soon enough. The morning after the battle, the shocking news of Ketchel's defeat flashed across the front pages of newspapers from east to west. If Ketchel had been in great condition, he might have recovered, and Papke knew it; a fact that he would have to face sooner than later as his plans to defend his title against Hugo Kelly in November fell through. With the Kelly fight canceled, Ketchel was the obvious choice for Papke's next opponent.

Even weeks after he defeated Ketchel, Papke kept insulting him in the newspapers with marked antagonism. Papke's comments become so frequent and acidic that a rumor began circulating that Papke had turned to insulting Ketchel's mother and family. Ketchel, who said little through the newspapers, was absolutely infuriated at the idea that Papke was insulting his family. In response to the supposed insults, Ketchel replied: "He insulted my mother. I'll kill the bastard!"

Willus Britt had a terrible time calming Ketchel, and Ketchel's supporters had taken to booing and shouting insults at Papke. The press thought that Papke beat Ketchel through a cowardly trick, and Britt was in agreement. As Ketchel seethed about Papke's insults, Britt seethed at the memory of Papke's cheap shot. Eventually, the memory of Papke's cheap shot proved more material than his insults toward Ketchel, and it was Ketchel who had to calm down Britt.

Britt called Papke's manager and issued a formal challenge, to which Papke didn't respond. Papke knew that his foul blow had been indispensable to his winning the match, and he also knew that, if he gave Ketchel another chance, Ketchel would have the advantage of being fueled by vengeance. According to ring etiquette, Ketchel was owed a rematch. But the problem was how to get Papke back into the ring. After brainstorming for a few days, Ketchel and Britt came up with a plan: Ketchel would vanish from the scene and reports would be spread that he was remorseful about losing his championship and had become an alcoholic. Meanwhile, as the newspapers continued to put pressure on Papke, accusing him of being a coward and not giving Ketchel another chance, Papke would be more likely to cave in and fight a supposedly alcoholic Ketchel.

As the plan was taking effect, Papke's appearance in public places had the effect of a rat scurrying into a powder room. People parted from his company as if he were diseased. An attention hound by nature, Papke found being a pariah unbearable and soon conceded to offer Ketchel a rematch. With the false reports of Ketchel's deterioration swirling through the papers, Papke began to feel overconfident and didn't train as hard as he had for the second match.

To Ketchel's surprise, the plan had worked. Britt soon settled negotiations with the Papke camp and the contracts were signed. Their third fight was set for Thanksgiving Day, 1908, at Jimmy Coffroth's Mission Street Arena. The rematch was announced across the country in the morning papers, and 16,000 thousand people would sell out the arena in four days.

Britt, Frank Rowen, John Roddy and Hype Igoe composed Ketchel's training crew, with Ketchel choosing heavyweight Bob Armstrong as his sparring partner. Armstrong was a skillful black prizefighter who would become a serious contender for the heavyweight championship, but would never get a shot at the title. The team bought train tickets and headed for Ketchel's training camp on his family's farm. With Britt taking an unusually serious view of Ketchel's upcoming match, Ketchel vanished from the limelight and started a brutal training regimen.

Every morning at seven o'clock, Ketchel would run or walk for miles and then take a two-hour swim in a lake with his siblings. In the afternoon, he did a three-hour workout and held competitive sparring sessions with Armstrong, ending with a long shower and a rubdown.

Ketchel took Sunday as a day of rest, relaxing and drinking fresh milk to calm the frenzy left over from his training.

When November arrived, Ketchel was in the best boxing shape of his life. But he wanted the boxing world to keep reading the false accounts of his self-demise until the day of his rematch. Just as Papke had surprised him with a cheap shot, Ketchel wanted to surprise Papke with his tremendous conditioning. Since the big event was set on Thanksgiving, Ketchel wanted his family to come to California and see the fight. On November 25th, Ketchel, his team and his family arrived at the Grand Rapids train station and headed for San Francisco. R.P. Dickerson, who arrived at the ranch a couple of days earlier, came too.

Ketchel made no excuses for his loss and was calm leading up to the rematch. But Britt sensed that Ketchel was still deeply angered and was ready to become a twice undisputed middleweight champion; a feat that had yet to be accomplished in Ketchel's time.

Chapter 13:
Ketchel vs. Papke III

By 2 p.m. on Thanksgiving Day, 1908, more than 15,000 fans had packed Jimmy Coffroth's Arena, and 6,000 people crowded the streets outside waiting for a blow-by-blow report that would be delivered by a special commentator. A large band played music at the arena's front entrance, and four large red, white and blue flags that said "Ketchel vs. Papke III" flapped in the breeze. It was glorious weather, and the fans that had seats at the top of the arena had a wonderful view of the bay. The Ketchel family got ringside seats and sat next to celebrities and political figures, with R.P. Dickerson and Ketchel's former manager, Joe O'Conner, sitting close by. Ketchel's most clamorous fans were women, and they seemed more eager for the fight to get started than the men. Just before Ketchel and Papke weighed in, Ketchel requested that they not weigh in at the same time in order to preserve the element of surprise that he had been planning. Ketchel weighed in at a solid 160 lbs., with Papke weighing in at 157 lbs. Legendary referee Jack Welsh would be the third man.

When Papke entered the ring a roar rumbled through the arena and boosted his already swelling confidence. A few minutes later, Ketchel came down the aisle in a robe, which everyone suspected hid a soft, shapeless physique. But when Ketchel and his team entered the ring and the robe came off, the crowd was amazed to see a ripped athlete in black trunks who was pumped and ready to go. Papke was shocked and turned away in embarrassment, realizing that he had been tricked.

Handing his robe to Britt, Ketchel walked over to Papke's corner and politely said: "We won't shake hands before, after or during the fight. You will be almost ready to shake hands with the undertaker when this fight is over. For ten rounds, I'll cut you to pieces and in the eleventh, I'll hit you so hard you won't be able to get up."

After the introductions and fight poses for the cameras, both men were called to the center of the ring for final instructions. Ketchel continued taunting Papke.

"It took you 12 rounds to stop a blind man. I am going to let your eyes stay open until the eleventh round. I want you to see me knock you out."

Papke kept up his confident behavior, but Ketchel could see that he was intimidated. After the brief instructions, Welsh ordered both men to go back to their corners and await the bell. Britt told Ketchel to kill Papke and wished him good luck. Pete Stone and Bob Armstrong did the same. The crowd stood as they anxiously awaited the first bell. As round one opened, Ketchel raced out of his corner and a let out a scream as he landed the first damaging blow; a deadly left hook to Papke's jaw that had all of Ketchel's weight behind it. Papke dropped and slid across the ring from the force of the blow. He waited for the count of nine and then got to his feet. Within five seconds of the first bell, Papke was sent to the canvas, his jaw broken in three places.

From round one to the fight's conclusion, Ketchel put on one of the best performances of his career, making Papke look like a novice. He constantly drove powerful punches wrist deep into Papke's midsection and battered his ribcage. And in the second round, he made Papke's nose practically explode, busting it wide open with an incredible straight right. Inside of three rounds, Ketchel's entire body was covered in Papke's blood. By the sixth round, Papke had suffered several splintered ribs, giving his face with a look of horror every time Ketchel sent another punch to his midsection. Despite the intense punishment that he was receiving, Papke showed that he was game by repeatedly using his left jab to keep Ketchel off.

Everyone who watched the massacre knew that Ketchel could have ended it in far less time than he did. But he told Papke that the fight would last eleven rounds, and he meant it. As Ketchel continued to torture Papke, he kept repeating the words, "What did you say about my family...I'll Kill you!"

Papke eventually hit Ketchel below the belt and Ketchel complained to the referee, but his plea was ignored. Then, during a clinch, Ketchel gave the soon to be ex-champion a cold blooded warning: "The next time you pull another trick shot, I'll make sure the next punch ends your life." Papke didn't foul again.

At the opening of round eleven, Papke shocked everyone, including Ketchel, with his ability to put up a decent fight while being so injured. His face was beaten beyond recognition, and both of his eyes were swelled shut. He was bent over, using his left forearm to protect his damaged ribcage and his right glove to cover his jaw. He was soaked in blood from head to toe and had numerous lacerations to his forehead and face. Frequently, his body would convulse as he vomited blood during clinches. The champion looked like he had been run over by a tractor.

This fight was Ketchel at his meanest, for he wanted to humiliate

Papke as well as defeat him. In round eleven, Ketchel staggered Papke clear across the ring. Papke clinched and Ketchel furiously broke free, throwing a powerful, short left hook that landed squarely on Papke's broken jaw. This time, Papke couldn't stand any more and fell face forward, striking the mat with incredible force. Dazed, he arose and tried his best to back pedal and cover. But the punishment was taking its toll. Ketchel had a promise to keep and hammered away at Papke with a right to the body and a right to the head. When Papke's knees sagged, Ketchel put his famous shift into action, landing a heavy left hook to Papke's jaw that sent him to his hands and knees, from which he sank to the canvas. Jack Welsh tolled off a ten count, and then raised Ketchel's hand as the winner and new champion.

At the fight's conclusion, the arena crowd raced from their seats to get a closer look at The Michigan Assassin as he reunited with his belt. Britt hoisted Ketchel onto his shoulders and Ketchel waved and smiled at the crowd with his belt wrapped around his waist. After dismounting Britt's shoulders, Ketchel hugged his family and friends at ringside and prepared to leave the arena. Papke was rushed to a nearby hospital for immediate treatment of his wounds.

Ketchel became the first fighter to regain the crown of middleweight champion of the world. But Papke had almost set a record himself: his two months, two weeks and four days as middleweight champion was one of the shortest title reigns of all time. As in the case of Joe Thomas, Papke refused to believe that Ketchel was the better fighter, and bitterly protested that he had not heard the count by Jack Welsh. Papke's jaw was broken so badly that he had to talk through clenched teeth to complain about the fight to the press.

"I thought I was counted out unfairly. I heard referee Jack Welsh say 'six' and then I heard him count 'eight.' I was waiting for 'nine', and the next thing I knew, they told me I had lost. I was ready to get up and fight some more, and I think I had a good chance to win."

Papke knew that, if he had continued, Ketchel might have killed him. Still, he made a string of excuses, grasping at straws to salvage his dignity. In fact, he was so distraught over the loss that he fired his long time manager, Tom E. Jones, hiring his brother, Eddie Papke, as his replacement. Like Ketchel in his first match with Papke, Papke had suffered his first knockout defeat. After leaving the hospital after two weeks, Papke's disfigurement was still severe enough that his own family had a hard time recognizing him. It was reported that when Papke's mother saw his face, she let out a scream and fainted.

Following Papke's one-sided loss, Britt would laugh every time Papke complained about the match to the *San Francisco Chronicle*. When Britt was asked in the press whether he thought that Papke would want to fight Ketchel again, he replied: "Of course, this is not the last we'll see of Papke. He'll be dumb enough to fight Ketchel again, which is no more problem for Stan or me, but one thing is for sure: I bet you Billy won't talk about Stanley's mother again."

After celebrating his win over Papke for a few weeks, Ketchel was ready to head to his parents' farm to celebrate Christmas. On Wednesday, December 23, Ketchel arrived in Grand Rapids laden with gifts for his family. Michiganites had read about Ketchel's impending arrival in the papers, and hundreds of fans and reporters were waiting for him at the train depot. When Ketchel arrived, he was dressed in a neat black suit and a half-length brown overcoat. But his conservative look was shattered by a collection of immense diamonds that a jeweler had formed into a shirt front decoration. As he met his parents at the depot, Ketchel was kind to the press and indulged their questions, impressing them with his well-formed answers and causing them to notice that he rarely stood still.

At Christmas, Ketchel presented his brothers and father with impressive gifts. But he gave the best gifts to his mother, presenting her with a $1,000 bill that had been included in one of his fight winnings. He had also had a $200 gold piece made into a beautiful necklace, and had had expensive cloth prepared for the walls of the farmhouse. The Ketchel family had a wonderful holiday together, and Ketchel stayed until January 2, 1909.

Returning to San Francisco, Ketchel was looking forward to negotiating bigger fights.

With Papke out of the way, there wasn't a middleweight fighter that was capable of offering Ketchel a meaningful fight, except Tony Caponi of Chicago. However, Ketchel wanted to fight Caponi in Grand Rapids, and Caponi wanted to fight in Chicago. After a bitter debate, the fight plans fell through, and Caponi refused to fight Ketchel, which meant that Ketchel would be forced to fight heavyweights if he wanted a challenge. Initially, Britt thought that it was a crazy idea. Yet, at the same time, he had visions of making Ketchel heavyweight champion, as numerous boxing experts had attested that Ketchel's punch was definitely strong enough to compete. As the idea gained momentum, Ketchel increasingly believed in the experts' opinions.

"Why not?" he reasoned. "You hit the big ones right and they'll go out as quick as the little ones."

Britt's master plan to seat Ketchel on the richest throne in boxing started in New York City in the spring of 1909, and he would select the physically imposing, clever, one time light heavyweight champion, Jack O'Brien, as Ketchel's first heavyweight opponent. Three weeks later, Caponi finally decided that he would face Ketchel in Grand Rapids. Once Britt and Ketchel got word of Caponi's announcement, they immediately signed a contract for a three-round exhibition fight at the Old Powers Theater. Ketchel knew that he should have fought Caponi a long time ago, and he wanted to get the match over with before facing Jack O'Brien.

Chapter 14:
Ketchel vs. Caponi and O'Brien

Ketchel's exhibition with Caponi took place on January 15, 1909. According to the *Grand Rapids Herald*, the total gate was $1,700. Ketchel was boxing for cheap. As middleweight champion, he typically requested purses of $7,000 or $8,000 a fight. But the fact that the bout was only three rounds and would take place in his hometown had moved him to fight for less. Ketchel appeared in the ring wearing a multicolored bathrobe, an old tan cap and had an American flag draped around his waist to indicate his championship. But despite his eclectic appearance and the palpable excitement of his hometown fans, the fight would be a lackluster event. Caponi, a boxer who thrived on technique, would make Ketchel look clumsy and give him a bloody nose. "Ketchel fought like he was in a trance. I don't see how he ever beat Papke," said one ticket holder. Caponi also issued a disparaging comment about Ketchel. He told reporters that, even though it was an exhibition, Ketchel tried hard to knock him out. "He was throwing punches as hard as he could," Caponi said.

Ketchel laughed when he heard Caponi's statement. "Why it was nothing at all. I didn't hurt him but merely tried to make it interesting to the crowd."

Later, Ketchel told Britt that he would never fight another exhibition. A good boxer could always make a natural fighter, such as himself look bad, he said. The following is a clip from a 1909 edition of the *Grand Rapids Herald* that described Ketchel's brief bout with Caponi, beginning with the evening's first match of Eddie Nelson versus Charley Doxtator:

> That there was to be fighting, but simply an exhibition bout was made clear by referee Lynch in the semi windup, when he sent Eddie Nelson and Charley Doxtator to their corners when they cut loose at a pretty hot clip. Doxtator refused to continue after the rebuke and his gloves were taken off. This action on the part of Lynch created a great difference of opinion in the house. But among those who worked their think tanks it was apparent that it was all that could have been done. The greater number of spectators came for the purpose of seeing Stanley Ketchel in action and this was the main attraction. Had Lynch done other wise it is doubtful whether Ketchel would have been seen in the ring. A cordon of police was on hand to see that the affair was conducted according to a letter of the city of Grand Rapids and had Nelson and Doxtator gone along in the style in which they started, with bad blood apparent, the bout would have surely been stopped. This would have meant disappointment as far as Ketchel and Caponi were concerned. In the second he stopped Ketchel with a couple of blows to the nose that tipped the champ back on his heels, and this ability to reach through Ketchel's guard showed that Caponi has ability in the fighting game that he makes in his desire for a match with Billy Papke or Hugo Kelly. Ketchel however, kept putting the pressure on Caponi, rushing his opponent and the blows that he landed

were mostly from close range and this infighting was one of the spectacular kinds. One of Ketchel's favorite efforts besides the "shift" is a head straightener that he lands by getting his fist to his opponents jaw. Jamming his head back on his shoulders by throwing his whole body into the air. A couple of those blows sent Caponi's head snapping back. Then the famous "Ketchel shift" on the lead, with a right brought into play, was shown. Ketchel has used this move with better results than any other fighter. With the exception of Bob Fitzsimmons, he landed it on Caponi in the third round last night with much steam, and for a moment the blow to the pit of the stomach had the Italian in despair. Both boxers were clever in their footwork. Caponi repeatedly got out of the way of Ketchel's rushes, but once or twice was sent dangerously near the ropes. Ketchel was the aggressor at all times, continually keeping after his opponent putting on pressure. In the first round Caponi landed a blow on Ketchel, then bored in keeping his blows directed at the body, working in a couple of shifts that landed his left and some jaw pushers of his jump variety. Caponi covered all of Ketchel's punches directed at his head, but slipped and went to his knees in an effort to duck Ketchel's forceful rushes. Then Ketchel crowded him somewhat and several clinches resulted. In these Ketchel got a few taps to the Italian's middle regions. Tony sent in a couple to the champ's nose that straightened him up. The third session was faster than anytime of the fight. Then it was that Ketchel slipped his right hand to Caponi's body on a shift and distressed him. He let up his rushing. However, but had he wished he could easily have finished Caponi then and there. The fighters were cheered as they went to their dressing rooms and those spectators who wanted to see Ketchel in a typical exhibition of fighting style were satisfied.

The following day, Ketchel had nothing but praise for Caponi: "I believe he is far cleverer than either Hugo Kelly or Billy Papke. I know he was in perfect condition last night, and I've seen them all in the same style, and Caponi has them stopped. He landed blows on me last night that had been in a finish fight instead of an exhibition would have bothered me greatly. All that I hope is that I have a chance to meet him on the west coast or other places where we can go to it as hard as we want to."

Caponi also had a comment on Ketchel and wanted a rematch with the champion: "I let Ketchel set the pace all the way, but I surely would like to meet him again. I do not think he could land that left of his on me with his style of fighting and he is willing to try it out in a longer battle."

Caponi and Ketchel would meet again, but not for a while. Ketchel's next fight would take place in Schenectady, New York, against O'Brien. A few weeks after the Grand Rapids exhibition, thousands of New York City boxing fans were anxiously waiting their turn to see Ketchel in the flesh. Ketchel received the news of his pairing with O'Brien in a March 26, six-round match at The National Sporting Club in New York City while he was in Chicago, attending an auto show with his friends Jimmy Hagen and Pete Stone. Although Ketchel would have liked more than six rounds, especially against boxer as clever O'Brien, he figured that he could make up for the fight's brevity by boxing at a fast clip. Ketchel wasn't bothered in the least by the suggestion that he would have a difficult time making weight for the fight:

> I believe I can take off weight more easily than any other man in the ring today. I will post money for the weight, and it's the safest thing, you know that I will make the 158. Why, when I fought Papke first time they talked a lot about me not making the weight and called me a damn fool and a lot of other pet names, because I went against all rules of training to reduce my weight by drinking all the milk I wanted throughout the working period. I made the weight

didn't I? It will be easy for me to make the 158, although to do it I'll have to lose something like 25 pounds in three weeks. While I'll go below the mark and be coming back by the time I land on the scales in New York. Then there'll be something like seven or eight hours to keep on going up after the weighing. I'll get back to 165 by that time probably. This bout with O'Brien gives me chance to get into the ring again and get what is to me good money. I've been panned hard for not going on stage or getting into the moving picture business to pick up easy money. They say I have the looks for a leading man but I won't accept theatrical engagements, although I've had many offers to go out with the shows. Other fighters may fancy the footlights, but not me. I like to see a good show or hear good musicians once in a while, but that lets me out. I'd rather go back to cow punching and mining than being an actor fighter. You know I may be a bit of a crank on some subjects but I've never seen a horse race or a professional baseball game. They have no attractions for me whatsoever. I like keeping to myself. I intend to leave for the big city very soon probably early next week with my manager Willus Britt to meet O'Brien.

In Early March, Ketchel's team traveled to New York City in an expensive luggage car. Ketchel stayed busy entertaining Britt with vivid accounts of his days and nights spent riding the rails as hobo. The stories perfectly juxtaposed what he had become. Instead of a scrappy hobo, he was now a well-loved boxing star that sat before Britt clad in "purple and fine linen." Nonetheless, there was a homespun glamour about the old days that still had a grip on Ketchel, his eyes lighting up as he lounged in the luxurious atmosphere of the Pullman, recounting his days of poverty with a black cigar clenched between his teeth. He told Britt, who had never experienced the hobo life or answered the call of the open road, that he had never been so happy as when he was broke, and wouldn't care if he had it all to do over again.

The New York sports fraternity greeted Ketchel with open arms as he disembarked the train. Hundreds of fans were waiting at the depot for Ketchel's arrival, and Britt would try to capitalize on their curiosity. Later that night, at Britt's suggestion, Ketchel was decked out in a dapper cowboy outfit that made him look everything like a dashing prizefighter. On the Broadway scene, he sipped imported champagne and smoked cigars in the company of choirgirls and other nightlife characters. Ketchel enjoyed his time in social New York immensely. He loved the bright lights, the homage of the crowds and the feeling that he was the center of attention wherever he appeared. He would race up and down the highways in a bright yellow roadster with his personal secretary, Billy Silver, riding shotgun. He was living in a world of dangerous rapture, of which he said: "these things make existence tolerable."

But Ketchel had to settle down and get in shape if he wanted to beat O'Brien. The weight agreement for Ketchel's fight with Philadelphia Jack was set at 158 pounds, give or take two pounds. On the afternoon of March 26, 1909, both men tipped the scales at 2 p.m. inside the National Sporting Club. O'Brien was surprised when he met Ketchel, finding him not as he had expected.

"Mr. Ketchel, I'm happy to meet you," said the gentlemanly O'Brien as he strode across the room to shake Ketchel's hand. "I didn't know you were so young and good looking. Your remarkably fine record deceived me."

"Hello Jack, how are you?" returned Ketchel. "I've heard a lot about you and I hope we give the crowd a great show."

Both Ketchel and O'Brien were in superb condition and weighed in at a solid 160 pounds. As fighting time approached, the arena filled with thousands of fans, with numerous celebrities sitting ringside. A large group from Philadelphia, including the mayor and other public officials, came to root for O'Brien. In his corner, O'Brien had as one of his seconds A.J. Drexel Biddle, scion of one of America's oldest and best-known families at the time. Kid McCoy, Jack Eagan, Johnny Rohan and Jack Hanlon also were in his corner. Britt, Pete Stone, Bob Armstrong, Jimmy Johnston, Jimmy Frayne and Hype Igoe handled Ketchel.

While Ketchel was lying on a cot in his dressing room, waiting to be called into the arena, a messenger boy delivered a telegram. Ketchel read the wire, folded it up carefully and kissed the paper. There were tears filling his eyes, and Pete Stone, who sitting on the edge of the cot, inquired if Ketchel had received bad news. Ketchel shook his head.

"No" he said with emotion. "Nothing like that. It's just a few words from my mother in Detroit, wishing me good luck, but somehow it always gets me when I hear from her, or think about her. She was always so good to me."

Of the thousands of people who witnessed the fight, a majority of them would go on to say that it was one of the most thrilling fights in New York boxing history. O'Brien, the boxing master who had whipped the best heavyweights for 14 years, was facing the hard-hitting, energetic Michigan Assassin. The contrast between the two fighters as they came to the center of the ring for Referee Tim Hurst's instructions was striking. Ketchel, with his flaring red trunks and well-rounded build, was the personification of youth and vitality, while O'Brien appeared pale, grim and resolved. Ketchel laughed and moved as his seconds were putting on his gloves. O'Brien, too, was smiling, but it was a stern smile that seemed born of experience.

Hours before the fight, Britt and Tim Hurst kept telling Ketchel: "O'Brien is too clever for you to rush him, box him don't fight him."

Other friends advised Ketchel to change his style for the O'Brien fight as well. Initially, Ketchel refused, citing the fact that he was a fighter and not a fancy boxer. But under mounting pressure from Britt, he finally gave in, and the decision was a mistake for eight rounds.

In round one, Ketchel came out of his corner with a rush and got the fight off to a quick pace. But O'Brien met his charges with terrific left jabs and displayed excellent footwork. Ketchel was a master of cutting off the ring and made sure that O'Brien didn't have enough room to circle around. But O'Brien would quickly step in and catch Ketchel with a left hook as Ketchel tried to rush him after cutting off the ring. Near the end of the round, Ketchel planted a big left hook to the ribcage and O'Brien's legs buckled as the bell rang. O'Brien complained to the referee about the punch, asserting that Ketchel's body shot was low. But O'Brien knew that the punch wasn't a foul and complained to make Ketchel more cautious with his powerful body shots.

In round two, O'Brien slipped, sidestepped, ducked and blocked while delivering an assault of straight jabs followed by hooks, uppercuts and crosses. Despite bringing all of his ring skill into action, O'Brien couldn't stop Ketchel from reaching his body with cruel uppercuts to the stomach and heart. Near the end of the round, Ketchel caught O'Brien with a leaping left hook that sliced his eyelid open. Through the third, fourth and fifth rounds, both men were fighting desperately, with Ketchel landing well placed left hooks to O'Brien's body in an attempt to wear him down. Ketchel would easily slip inside his taller opponent and bury his fist in O'Brien's stomach, each time causing him to wince in pain.

When Ketchel was stunned by O'Brien's punches, he would snort and snarl like a wounded animal, lashing himself into a fury. Ketchel seemed to be getting stronger as the fight progressed, and his attacks were slowly wearing O'Brien down. By the sixth round, O'Brien had slashed Ketchel to ribbons, but O'Brien was no better off. His eyes and lips were cut, and huge red welts dotted his body. Going into the seventh round, Ketchel was well behind O'Brien on points. But the tide would suddenly turn. A series of body blows by Ketchel proved too painful for O'Brien, and he backed away in desperation. Then the bell rang, giving O'Brien a much needed rest. In round eight, O'Brien attempted a desperate rally but couldn't keep it up. Ketchel was after him, stalking and chasing him all over the ring. Suddenly, Ketchel delivered a right to O'Brien's heart that took O'Brien's breath away, dropping him for a nine count. Sensing the kill, Ketchel gave O'Brien everything that he had, but O'Brien was saved by the bell once more.

The fight was listed as a no decision bout, meaning that the only way it could be won was by knockout, and it was entering the final round. Because it could serve as an invaluable bargaining tool in future negotiations, Britt wanted a knockout in the worst way. But his desire would be foiled in the cruelest manner.

O'Brien wobbled out of his corner for the final three minutes with one idea: to stick it out. Ketchel was soon all over him, jabbing, hooking and rushing. But for the most part, O'Brien managed to cover his vulnerable points with his strong arms, leaving Ketchel to punch at little more than elbows and biceps. However, with six seconds left in the fight, Ketchel finally planted a blow that he had been trying to land all night. It was a perfectly timed right to O'Brien's jaw that carried all of the power that Ketchel could muster. Landing with a loud crack, the punch instantly sent O'Brien to the canvas, landing him flat on his back. The referee began his count. But on the count of four the bell sounded and the fight was over. The referee could have counted to 200 and O'Brien would have remained down. But since he couldn't reach a ten count, Ketchel technically failed to win the fight.

While no official verdict was given, the newspapers handed the victory to Ketchel. Under the rules of the New York State Athletic Commission, officials were required to render a verdict at the end of a fight, deciding either in favor of boxing quality by round or point score. As a result, the fight went into Richard K. Fox's record book as a ten-round no-decision bout with equal glory going to both fighters. Following his fight with O'Brien, Ketchel pleaded with Britt to get him a rematch in O'Brien's native Philadelphia. But Britt didn't want Ketchel to tangle with O'Brien again. He figured that a six-round contest was too short and would enable O'Brien to outbox Ketchel as he had done in the early part of their New York battle.

"Get me O'Brien," ordered Ketchel. "I don't care how many rounds we are scheduled to fight. I'll knock him out well within the distance this time. I would have put him away in our last fight if I hadn't followed your advice and Tim Hurst's. You both told me to box instead of fight, but next time I'll fight him off his feet."

In three months, Ketchel would have another go at O'Brien. But in the meantime, Britt had already set up negotiations for a six-round, no decision fight with up and coming middleweight, Hugh McGann, in Pittsburgh on May 18, 1909.

Chapter 15:
Ketchel vs. O'Brien II

Between his first and second matches with O'Brien, Ketchel faced off against Hugh McGann and Tony Caponi. Ketchel's no-decision fight with McGann was a dominating performance for Ketchel, seeing him easily pummel McGann and walk away in great condition. The following is a short account of Ketchel's match with McGann on May 18, 1909, from Portland, Maine's *Daily Advertiser*:

> Six Times tonight Hugh McGann was down for a count of nine in a six round bout with Stanley Ketchel, champion middleweight of the world. Five times in the sixth round, he was saved from a knockout in the second round. Twice he was knocked clear through the ropes across the press table into the seats of spectators. Ketchel apparently toyed with his opponent. Only the cheering voices of his champions from the audience inspired McGann several times to get upon his feet again, after being all but knocked out. For the first three rounds McGann fought hard and landed several times on the champion, but apparently he exhausted

himself in the early rounds and could not face the powerful blows of his antagonists after the first half of the bout. No decision was permissible under the Pennsylvania laws. Never before has so large an audience witnessed a boxing bout in Pittsburgh. Six thousand persons crowded Duquesne Gardens, among them being men prominent in financial, political and business circles. Preceding the big fight three preliminaries were pulled off. Both Ketchel and McGann were in prime condition.

Following Ketchel's lopsided defeat of McGann, he defeated Toni Caponi just as easily. According to the *Grand Rapids Herald*, Ketchel's June 2, non-title match against Caponi "lasted four rounds and both men fought before the American A.C. A crushing right to the jaw ruined everything for Caponi. The Chicagoan was a target for everything Ketchel threw. Tony was flattened once in the second round and four times in the fourth session. On the final knockdown he took the ten count at 1:26 of the fourth round."

In a span of five months, Ketchel had defeated Caponi twice, and he wouldn't fight him again. Just a short week later, he would be in Philadelphia for his rematch with O'Brien, which was the most anticipated fight in Philadelphia in 1909. On the day of the fight, Ketchel and O'Brien tipped the scales at the Old Scott House, located at the northeast corner of 15th and Filbert streets. Theodore Murphy weighed them at 3 p.m. sharp and recorded each fighter's weigh at 160 pounds. Murphy also was the proprietor of the Scott House, and was highly praised for his honesty in holding bets for big fights. Refereed by Jack McGuin, the ten-round match would take place at the Old National Sporting Club that was located just a few blocks from were O'Brien was born.

Over 13,000 people were outside and inside the clubhouse, and there were under cards before the main event. The first fight was between

Benny Kauffman and Sammy Smith, with Kauffman winning the battle easily. Ketchel's match with O'Brien got underway shortly after Kauffman and Smith left the ring, and the crowd was on its feet when O'Brien and Ketchel entered the ring. O'Brien emerged first and wore Irish green trunks with a red, white and blue belt. Ketchel entered the ring in his trademark red trunks, smirking as he basked in the applause. Britt kept reminding Ketchel that he had to force O'Brien into a brawl in order to defeat him. But Ketchel didn't need to be reminded. Pete Stone and Bob Armstrong were Ketchel's seconds.

After the customary handshake and the opening bell, Ketchel immediately went after O'Brien with tenacity, landing a left to O'Brien's body before he could cover up. Ketchel then missed a straight right to O'Brien's jaw. But he immediately came back with a straight right to O'Brien's body that hit with a thud. O'Brien countered with a right to the jaw, but Ketchel seemed unphased as he waded in and, breaking from a clinch, opened a massive cut over O'Brien's right eye. O'Brien appeared off kilter and nervous, missing with his reliable left jab again and again. But he eventually landed two left jabs to Ketchel's face before Ketchel chased him back on the defensive. Ketchel then missed a hard left hook to the head. But he again delivered the same punch to O'Brien's body as the bell rang.

At the beginning of round two, Ketchel raced out of his corner with a rush, chasing O'Brien to the ropes. O'Brien countered with a left to the face and then delivered a light left and right combination to Ketchel's head, causing O'Brien's hometown fans to yell in approval. Then he repeated the combination and the uproar grew louder. Despite the crowd's impression that O'Brien was seriously compromising Ketchel, Ketchel continued to push O'Brien around the ring as he pleased. He delivered a hard right to O'Brien's stomach and followed it with a wicked right hand to the jaw that sent O'Brien to the canvas for a nine count. After assuming his feet, O'Brien was soon on the canvas again as Ketchel hit him with a right to the body and a left hook to the jaw. But he was saved from defeat by the bell.

At the outset of round three, Ketchel again leapt from his stool with a bound, rushing the weakened, wobbly O'Brien to the ropes, who managed to slightly elude Ketchel's onslaught and deliver some weak blows to Ketchel's face. Ketchel pushed past O'Brien's jabs and hit him with walloping right and left hooks to the body that sent him staggering toward the ropes. Pursuing O'Brien at the ropes, Ketchel delivered a hard right to the jaw and gave O'Brien his third trip to the canvas. Ketchel walked away as if the fight were over as the referee started his count, and he soon waved Ketchel to his corner as an indication that the fight was over. O'Brien managed to get to his feet after the fight was called, but he was barely able to walk without assistance. A day later, O'Brien decided that Ketchel was the world's best boxer, giving the following statement to the press:

> Stanley Ketchel is the greatest fighter the ring has today. Though not the proud possessor of the heavyweight title, he is by far a better man than Jack Johnson, and if they ever meet Ketchel will stop Jack inside of 10 rounds. The Michigan scrapper accomplished something last night when he forced the referee McGuigan to end the fight in the third round to save me from bodily harm and that defeat of a knockout than no other living fighter can boast of and he did the job up in decisive style. I probably have more battles in my career than any man who ever donned a glove, and I fought the toughest, but Ketchel is the head of the list. He has a harder wallop than any man the ring ever possessed, and his nerve or gameness is undying. In his hands I was as helpless as a child and I believe I am the master of six round fighting. I have staved off many a great fighter, clever ones, hard hitting ones and ones that had both, but they were not

the equal of Ketchel. There are talks of a Ketchel – Johnson battle for October 16, and Johnson had $5,000 posted as a forfeit for appearance. My tip to Johnson is to stay away from Ketchel if he wants his title."

Nat Fleischer was in Quakertown to cover Ketchel's rematch with O'Brien for the New York press and was at Green's Hotel when Ketchel arrived to check in for a room. He walked over to the telegraph desk and asked for a blank.

"Can I help you, Stan," Nat inquired, being aware of Ketchel's limited written English.

"Yes, I want to send a telegram to pop in Detroit. Just write: I won the fight, Stanley. "What fight?" Fleischer asked in astonishment.

"The fight with O'Brien tonight," Ketchel replied.

"Why, that doesn't take place until four hours from now. It's only six o'clock."

"What's the difference?" Ketchel replied with a smile. "I always telegraph the old man before I go into the ring. He likes to know, so I tell him. It always comes out as I say."

Ketchel had a good time in Philadelphia for the next week or so and then returned to Grand Rapids to train for his fourth and final meeting with the persistent Billy Papke. Negotiations were already set for the fight to occur on the fifth of July. In light of Ketchel's lack of down time, one of his closest friends, Hype Igoe, begged him to take a rest.

"Go up to Vancouver or down to Hot Springs. Catch your breath before you collapse." But Ketchel wasn't in the mood to relax. He had become the hottest boxing draw since Jim Jeffries was heavyweight champion, and he wanted to do away with Billy Papke and set his sights on new horizons.

Chapter 16:
Ketchel vs. Papke IV

"I'm going to let Papke have another chance in July. He may catch me with one of his wallops, but I think I've got his measure and will win inside of ten rounds, for I'll be bigger and better than ever before." **Stanley Ketchel, 1909**

After a few weeks of training at his family's farm, Ketchel, his father and his brothers traveled to Colma, California, for Ketchel's fourth meeting with Billy Papke. By this time, Ketchel had started bathing in salt brine to make his skin taut, and it made his face look grim and fierce. Many fighters during Ketchel's era used salt brine so their skin wouldn't scar, but Ketchel's hardened appearance, combined with his womanizing and general pursuit of night life caused his friends to worry about his health. Three weeks before the fight, Ketchel had developed a hacking cough from his cigar habit, and he looked drawn and pale. In light of his cough, Britt sent Ketchel to one of San Francisco's best doctors. According to rumor, the doctor treated Ketchel for syphilis. Even after

Ketchel's medical treatment, Britt felt that it might be best if the fight with Papke were postponed, but Ketchel wouldn't hear of it.

Another alarming characteristic that Ketchel began displaying around this time was a hair trigger temper. His mood swings became unpredictable and his double-sided personality often proved dangerous to others, especially if he was behind the wheel of a car. Ketchel's closest associates were convinced that something was wrong, but were nervous about approaching him, fearing that it would throw him into a rage. In 1909, syphilis was a fatal disease and, like today, caused mental deterioration. Whether Ketchel had Syphilis isn't known. But in any case, his apparently compromised health wasn't going to stand in the way his fighting Papke. It was Papke's last chance to show that he was truly on Ketchel's level, and he was going to make the most of it.

After the opening bell of his fourth go around with Papke, Ketchel smashed Papke in the stomach and, after some wrestling, duplicated the blow. Then, breaking from a clinch, Ketchel gave Papke a left uppercut to the jaw, and proceeded to deliver a succession of right and left hooks to the body and head that made Papke seek another clinch. By the end of the round, Ketchel was already at a clear advantage.

In round two, Ketchel and Papke fought entirely at close range, with Ketchel constantly forcing Papke against the ropes. Locked in a clinch with Papke and against the ropes, Ketchel suddenly shot a fearful uppercut to Papke's jaw and then ripped a similar blow to Papke's stomach. Papke retaliated with a vicious left to Ketchel's jaw. The round ended with Ketchel and Papke still fighting at close quarters.

At the outset of round three, Ketchel rushed Papke against the ropes and would continue to do so throughout the round. While against the ropes, Papke delivered two right body punches and then fought Ketchel to the center of the ring. Papke landed a wicked left to the jaw and soon afterward drove a right and a left to Ketchel's stomach. Ketchel then landed a straight right to Papke's mouth and blood oozed through Papke's lips as he took his corner at the sound of the bell. Ketchel opened the fourth round with a fearful left hook to Papke's jaw. Then he landed right and left hooks to the jaw and body. Ketchel planted a straight right over the heart, but Papke only smiled. The round ended with a slight advantage to Ketchel.

At the opening of round five, Ketchel met Papke's rush with a straight left jab to the jaw and they clinched. Throughout the round, Referee Roche exhausted himself prying them apart. But after breaking from the clinches, Ketchel would typically go on the offensive, at one point forcing Papke through the ropes by sheer strength and nearly following him over. At the beginning of round six, Papke hit Ketchel in the jaw with a right uppercut, sending Ketchel's head backward. They fought so fiercely that, at one point, they fell to the floor from their exertions. After regaining their feet, Ketchel planted two lefts and a right to Papke's head, breaking his right hand in the process. Immediately afterward, Ketchel shot two short arm lefts to Papke's jaw and forced him against the ropes, where he put in three body punches. The round ended in a vicious but ineffectual rally. Ketchel had a slight advantage.

In round seven, Ketchel and Papke went at each other tenaciously, but most of the blows flew harmlessly through the air. Eventually, Ketchel forced Papke against the ropes, delivering a left uppercut to the body. Papke then landed a right to the face, and Ketchel retaliated with a left shift to the stomach. As the round ended, it appeared to be a draw. In round eight, Ketchel quickly landed a right and a left to the body, forcing Papke to clinch. After some fruitless exchanges, Papke gave Ketchel an uppercut to the chin, leaving him partly covered in blood as the round ended. In round nine, Ketchel rushed in and swung a vicious right to Papke's head and got an equally hard punch to the face in return. Then he hooked a vicious right to that jaw that brought blood streaming from Papke's mouth. Ketchel was looking to land a vital punch, and he fought Papke to a neutral corner where he landed two wallops to the face as the bell rang. It was Ketchel's best round so far.

In round ten, Papke surprised Ketchel by landing a couple of stiff face punches. But Ketchel instantly shot a right and a left to Papke's jaw with merciless precision, making it look as if he would put the Thunderbolt on the mat. However, Papke managed to hang on and was eventually saved by the bell. Despite the beating he had taken at the end of round ten, Papke emerged with a burst of new energy in round eleven. Ketchel hit him with right and left hooks, to which Papke responded with a full left swing to Ketchel's jaw. As Ketchel went after his man, delivering blow after blow to Papke's jaw, he slipped to the floor, his foot catching on Papke's shoe tops. He was up immediately and waded in relentlessly, but he was unable to land a knock out punch.

In round 12, Ketchel drove a hard right to Papke's jaw that sent Papke against the ropes. After Ketchel sent a hard right to Papke's face, Papke came at him, landing vicious left and right punches to the jaw that staggered Ketchel. The crowd rose to its feet in an uproar and shouted for the underdog. Ketchel, however, was not stopped. He exchanged punch for punch, ending the round in a draw. In round 13, Papke's biggest moment came when he landed a vicious right to Ketchel's jaw, causing him to clinch. But Ketchel soon responded with his own right to the jaw, for which he was rebuked by a right uppercut to the chin. Papke seemed to be taking confidence as the battle progressed, and when the round closed, he had a slight advantage.

By the opening of round 14, the fighters were so covered in blood that the spectators couldn't see their faces. They fought at a lighting quick pace for a minute and a half, but only one blow—a right to the body—landed on Ketchel. Ketchel then hit Papke with a forceful right to the body, causing Papke to clinch. The rest of the round was fought at close range, with Papke emerging with a slight advantage. Ketchel opened round 15 with a vicious left chop to Papke's jaw, a moment later sinking a left into Papke's stomach and forcing him against the ropes. The men clinched, wrestled and stalled, and then slowed up perceptibly. At close range, Papke swung short arm rights and lefts to the jaw until the bell rang, ending a tame round.

In round 16, the men battled at a furious clip at close quarters. Again and again, they hooked each other with right and left combinations, but without much result. Breaking from a clinch, Ketchel gave Papke an uppercut to the jaw, but Papke responded with a left to the body, which he improved upon with a straight left to Ketchel's face. The fighters were locked in each other's embrace as the bell rang. Round 17 saw each contestant lose punching power. But towards the end of the round, Papke suddenly shot a stiff left to the pit of Ketchel's stomach, which Ketchel quickly countered with a left to the body and a good left hook to the jaw. Then Papke staggered Ketchel with a straight left to the jaw as the bell rang.

In round 18, after considerable wrestling and clinching, Papke drove a nasty right straight to Ketchel's jaw and broke his right hand in the process. Papke forced Ketchel against the ropes, putting in two weak lefts to the face. Then he jarred Ketchel with two forceful left hooks to the jaw. Ketchel spat blood and appeared to weaken, but he managed to brace and shoot two solid lefts to Papke's jaw as the bell rang. In round 19, Ketchel came out dancing and they waltzed into a clinch. Throughout most of the round, Ketchel and Papke contented themselves with clinching and staying close. But after two minutes of uneventful fighting, Papke suddenly shot a right to Ketchel's jaw that sent him staggering halfway across the ring, which Papke followed with another vicious clip to the chin before the bell sounded.

In round 20, both men exhausted their strength at close range. Ketchel fought desperately to land a telling punch, and Papke rocked his head with two rights to the chin in quick succession. Ketchel rushed Papke against the ropes, seeking vainly to land a crucial blow, but Papke smothered his attempts. Ketchel continued to rush Papke around the ring with the force of his body, and the round ended with Papke in a neutral corner. To Papke's surprise, the referee promptly declared Ketchel the victor on points. The decision was received with cheers mingled with shouts. But regardless of the crowd's opinion, the Ketchel-Papke series was finally over.

Ketchel knew that the most lucrative bouts were in the heavyweight division, and he was determined to make it beyond the light heavyweight division. It wouldn't be long until the whole country would know that Ketchel was setting his sights on the new heavyweight champion of the world, Jack Johnson.

Chapter 17:
Ketchel vs. Johnson

On December 26, 1908, Jack Johnson became the first African-American heavyweight champion when he defeated Tommy Burns in Rushcutter's Bay near Sydney Australia in a stadium that was erected for the fight. After Johnson taunted the Canadian fighter and gave him a tremendous beating, he won on a technical knockout in the fourteenth round. Burns had been heavyweight champion from 1906–1908, and had set a record for the most consecutive title defenses: eleven. White society was outraged at Burns's defeat, and Johnson rubbed salt in the wound by flaunting his wealth and showing off his golden smile. Almost immediately following Burns's defeat, the search was on for a "great white hope" to reclaim the heavyweight title.

In 1909, Ketchel would be Johnson's first match following Johnson's arrival as heavy weight champ. But the white public were disappointed when they read in the papers that there wasn't any animosity between Ketchel and Johnson; a fact that led to some controversy for Ketchel.

"I have no hate toward Johnson," Ketchel explained. "Like I said before, I just want to make it clear that my upcoming fight with him is not a 'white hope' battle in my mind's eye. But if the boxing public wants it that way then so be it, it's their problem, not mine. I'm a huge attraction from California to New York...and I feel I have a right to express my feelings about this search for a white hope to topple Johnson. In my opinion the search is absolutely daffy. I've worked with black employees during my time at the Witticomb furniture factory with my father and we made friends readily."

For the white public, a white fighter respecting Johnson's boxing ability was one thing. But the idea of his being friends with Johnson was quite another. For Ketchel, the latter put a temporary blemish on his career and caused some of his fans to defect. When Ketchel praised Johnson to the press, many of his statements were unmentioned or altered in the newspapers. As for Johnson, he wasn't taking his match with Ketchel seriously; he was merely willing to participate. He had seen Ketchel fight a few times and remembered his style, thinking of him as a little boxer with tremendous nerve. But he knew that he wasn't going to be defeated by another boxer's nerve; he was too powerful and skilled for that.

Leading up to Ketchel's match with Johnson, Thomas Edison's Kinetoscope was fascinating audiences across the United States by showing moving pictures. As a result, the public was eager to have Ketchel's match with Johnson filmed and shown in movie theaters. Ketchel and Johnson were intrigued by the idea, and they started debating whether their match would be a real fight or an exhibition match. After much conversation, Ketchel and Britt decided to do an exhibition match and pick up some easy money. But deep down, Ketchel looked at the match as more than a strange pit stop in the midst of his middleweight career. He had always dreamed of becoming heavyweight champion, even though he wasn't blessed with the physical qualifications.

As Ketchel's match with Johnson drew closer, fiction became confused with fact. Even today, some argue the existence of a pre-fight deal between Ketchel and Johnson, referring to it as "the double cross", suggesting that Johnson fought in the spirit of an exhibition match while Ketchel didn't. But such ideas typically subsist on confusion over post fight statements issued by both camps. Following the fight, Johnson said that the match was never meant to be anything more than an exhibition and that "heavy artillery" was not to take place, but that Ketchel had violated this agreement. But the most reliable view of the situation comes from Ketchel's friend, Hype Igoe, who sat in on both preliminary meetings between Johnson, Ketchel and Britt:

> In Both meetings Britt did most of the talking. He was bold, direct and sincere. He told Johnson that he had no intention of allowing Ketchel to engage in a free for all with him (Johnson) and that his sole objective was money. He proposed a 20 – round exhibition to be held at Jimmy Coffroth's Colma, California arena with good seats to go about $25. He proposed that neither man open up with "heavy punches" and that the fight run it's full course, at the conclusion of which Johnson would retain his heavyweight championship since no decision could be rendered according to law. Additional money will be yielded to the movie rights. Johnson's face gave way to his famous golden smile as he rose to his impressive 6 feet 4 inches and extended his hand to Britt at the close of the first meeting. He said he would give the proposition careful thought and suggested a second meeting in New York City three weeks hence. In New York's Wentworth Hotel, on September 25, 1909, Ketchel and Johnson signed contracts before a maze of reporters. Ketchel wore an overly sized padded coat and cowboy boots with large heels to diminish the size difference when posing with Johnson before dozens of cameras. Then, after the mob left, they sealed their private deal with Britt raising a toast.

In leaving, Johnson slapped Britt gently on the back and said: 'Mr. Willus, at last I found an honest man.'

Leading up to the fight, Ketchel tried to add an air of excitement to his bout with Johnson by telling reporters, "I can lick Johnson. But at the pace he's living that's no great trick." But Ketchel himself was still drawn and pale, and was continually coughing according to some. Prior to mentioning Johnson's love of fast living to the press, Ketchel had staggered back to his California training camp after a wild binge in San Francisco. In truth, both Ketchel and Johnson were burning the candle at both ends, but Ketchel's candle was burning the fastest. Despite his dedication to nightlife, Johnson was still a remarkable specimen. Preceding their match, Johnson pulled up to Ketchel's camp in his handmade racecar. Wrapped around his considerable bulk was a 20–pound driving coat that he had picked up in Australia. Johnson and Ketchel split a bottle of champagne brought by Johnson and sang songs together. After Johnson sped away in a cloud of dust, Ketchel said to Hype Igoe, "I certainly wish I coulda talked him out of that coat of his. I could use it to scare crows off my spread."

Two weeks later, under blazing sun in Colma, California, Johnson and Ketchel readied themselves to square off as the motion picture cameras rolled. Johnson was 31 years old and weighed in at 205 pounds, while the 22-year-old Ketchel weighed in at only 170. Ketchel entered the ring first wearing his usual red trunks. In his corner were Willus Britt, Frankie Lohrman, Pete Stone and Bob Armstrong. In Johnson's corner were trainer and corner man, Harry Foley, and Johnson's manager, George Little. Johnson shook Ketchel's hand and walked back to his corner, awaiting the bell and as he stood smiling and showing his famous gold teeth. He wore long green trunks with a flag wrapped around his waist that served as a belt. After quick introductions by

Billy Jordan, a short photograph session and instructions by referee Jack Welch, both men were anxious to get started.

The 20-round bout began with Johnson sending a hard left to Ketchel's stomach, which Ketchel absorbed without flinching. He was happy to see Johnson lead, as he wanted a chance to counter. But Johnson could read Ketchel like a book, anticipating his moves well before he made them. Johnson never stood still, was constantly jabbing and dodged the majority of Ketchel's punches. The first ten rounds were all Johnson, and it was evident that he was toying with Ketchel. But since Johnson made Ketchel's nose his primary target, it was broken and gushed blood. At the sight of Ketchel's nose, Britt felt that Johnson was making the match more than an exhibition. But if he were, he would eventually be repaid in round ten when Ketchel finally caught him with a solid right that landed high on Johnson's head. The blow made Johnson mad. But Ketchel should have been madder at Johnson's constantly thumping his broken nose. Ketchel and Johnson lost their footing and simultaneously fell to the mat midway through the tenth round, with Johnson drawing a roar from the crowd when he picked Ketchel up with one hand and set him upright. As the fight progressed, Ketchel managed to land some hard shots, but they didn't carry his full power, as he was still trying to make the match an exhibition.

As the minutes went by, Ketchel found it continually harder to cut his punches while the smiling Johnson threw punches that felt powerful. Britt had briefed Ketchel numerous times about fighting by the rules. He warned him to "pull his punches" and to move, move, move. But the roar of the crowd, his killer instinct and the frustration over almost a dozen rounds of "catching" had left him seething. When he stumbled back to his corner after a boring eleventh round, Britt sensed the gravity of the moment.

"I know what's going through that head of yours," Britt said.

"Forget It. Do like I say and keep moving. Don't throw no rocks, understand!"

Ketchel became angered with Britt and snapped back, "What the hell do you think I've been doing these past eleven rounds, Willus!"

With a swat to Ketchel's behind, Britt sent him out for round 12, not knowing what to expect. As the round opened, Ketchel suddenly rushed into a brief clinch with Johnson and sent a right to his jaw. Johnson fell flat on his back and seemed injured. But as Ketchel rushed at Johnson after Johnson resumed his feet, the crafty Johnson delivered a hard right to Ketchel's jaw and a quick left to his body. As Ketchel fell backward, Johnson sent another right to his face and Ketchel soon lay on the mat with blood gushing from his mouth. He made a weak effort to rise but fell down again. Johnson put his right hand on the rope, his left hand on his hip and listened for the fatal ten count, which soon arrived. Yet, despite Ketchel's defeat, he had achieved a measure of success against Johnson that other boxers hadn't. According to Hype Igoe:

> No one had ever tagged Johnson solidly with a right before, although a long list of artists had tried. Ketchel had the power of a man three times his size and Johnson dropped to the floor. The smile wiped off his face, Jack leaped to his feet. Ringsiders could sense the rage flashing through his mind. Ketchel, savage and snorting through his broken nose, came for forward for the kill. He was still coming when Johnson slugged him on the mouth with frightful force to end the fight. Stan wobbled over to Johnson's corner a few minutes later and congratulated him. What he had accomplished once, Stan figured he could do it again. But he took the chances of a novice. The experience he had gained in so many of his tough battles of the past should have made him act with caution before setting out on a new attack. But no, he rushed forth unguarded.

It took an hour before Ketchel fully recovered from Johnson's blows. A deep gash spouted blood from his lower lip where two of his teeth had impaled it. In the winner's dressing room, the two teeth were firmly embedded in the padding of Johnson's right glove.

"He can take some heavy blows," said Johnson, showing the press his left glove that was sodden with Ketchel's blood. "I must say though," Johnson continued, "he has given me a sorer chin than I ever had before."

After regaining his equilibrium, Ketchel said, "I am in better condition than Johnson now. Look at him; he is dazed. But for that one blow I would have beaten him."

Johnson heard about Ketchel's statement and said later, "He crossed me and I made him pay for it."

Johnson's handler pried Ketchel's teeth out of the champion's glove and sent them over to Ketchel's dressing room. There the cocky Ketchel shook them in his hand and rolled them out on a table, remarking to newspaper men: "Tell Johnson the point is 30 pounds, when I make it, I'm coming back and it will be a different story."

The Johnson fight was the climax and breaking point of Ketchel's career, and it would also be his last fight under Willus Britt's management, as well as his last fight in California.

Chapter 18:
Wilson Mizner, Franz Klaus and Sam Langford

Much has been said about how Ketchel's failure to defeat Johnson sent him into a depression, but it sent Britt into a depression as well. Ketchel and Britt went to Hot Springs, Arkansas, with their $27,465 purse to recover from the shock of Ketchel's loss. Ketchel soaked in hot baths all day to sooth his aching body and, according to one source, continued chasing women at night. He took to smoking opium instead of cigars, and one night the Arkansas police caught him smoking an opium pipe. Britt talked them out of pressing charges. Perhaps because he thought Ketchel's escalating wantonness was a sign that he would never see serious contention again, Britt decided to resign as his manager. But the official reason for Britt's resignation remains unclear. In any event, not long after giving up Ketchel, Britt was found passed out in a doorway in New York with poison in his pockets. The following is an account of Britt's near demise from a 1910 issue of the *Grand Rapids Herald*:

New York, March 31 - Willus Britt, former manager of Stanley Ketchel, the middleweight champion, who was taken to St. Vincent's hospital early today suffering from what is believed to have been poison, will probably recover. While his condition was serious at first he has improved so much that it was said at the hospital tonight that he would be discharged. Britt was found unconscious in a doorway in East Fourteenth Street by policeman Hand, who called Dr. Sullivan of St. Vincent's. Dr. Sullivan said Britt was suffering from alcoholism. In Britt's pocket five morphine tablets were found. At the hospital the surgeons made successful efforts to revive him. At first he could not speak. His eyes did not respond to the usual methods of Muscular contraction resorted to by the doctors.

Britt eventually recovered, but his health wouldn't last. He died in the spring of 1910 under mysterious circumstances. As for Ketchel, he soon began to feel that he still had some big fights left in him, and in late March 1910, he went under the management of legendary part-time writer and all around hustler, Wilson Mizner. Mizner was a gentleman who had sold stories to Hollywood and Broadway, booze to miners in the Yukon and tickets to testimonial dinners for himself. But Mizner was also a con man, and would borrow so much money from Ketchel that Ketchel couldn't afford to break from his management, even as Mizner amazingly attended no more than two of Ketchel's upcoming fights. When they came to together, Ketchel and Mizner began a search for a formidable middleweight challenger. Soon, a short and stocky brawler named of Frank Klaus was selected as Ketchel's next opponent, and Klaus accepted the challenge. Negotiations were set with Klaus's manager, George Engel, and the six-round fight would be held in Pittsburgh on March 23, 1910. The Duquesne Gardens Arena's 7,000 seats immediately sold out. Pittsburgh wanted to see Klaus win since it was his hometown.

Klaus had a record of 33 wins, 1 defeat, and 17 knockouts. As the fight was ready to begin, he entered the ring wearing white trunks with his manager at his side. Ketchel entered the ring in his red trunks along with Mizner, Pete Stone and Bob Armstrong. According to one report, Ketchel looked pale, drawn and far older than his 22 yrs. But regardless of what his appearance said about his health, he still talked like the Ketchel of old, never giving an inch to his opponents leading up to a fight. The following is an account of Ketchel's fight with Klaus from the *Grand Rapids Herald* shortly after the fight:

> While Ketchel did most of the leading Klaus was the more effective. At times both battlers were incredibly cautious, much to the disappointment of the crowd. The second and third sessions were very rough with a lot of infighting involved. Ketchel slipped to the canvas in the fourth round getting away from Klaus and Frank helped his opponent get back on his feet. The fifth round was a huge round for Klaus landing many right hand counters to Ketchel's chin. By this time the "Michigan Assassin" was already fatigued and looked very drawn and during the clinches he started gasping for breath. Ketchel's fighting style seemed eroded through out the fight until the sixth and final round when Ketchel finally found himself. Stanley came back to life and tore into his rival as of old and tried hard to put Klaus away. There were fighting in a furious pace as the bell rang ending the affair. Since it was a No-Decision fight and no knockout nobody won. Many ringsiders agreed that a draw would have been a good verdict had one been rendered. Frank Klaus would move on to have a successful ring career with many legendary fighters including – Billy Papke, Jack Dillion, Porky Flynn, Georges Carpentier and future middleweight champion and Pittsburgh native Harry Greb in 1918. A couple of days later the Pittsburgh public was very disappointed and had had enough of Stanley Ketchel. Cancel date on Ketchel for another bout in Pittsburgh Pa.

March 25, 1910 – Fight promoters of this city are through with Stanley Ketchel as far as fights are concerned. This was made public here today, when Pittsburgh Athletic Club canceled the date for Ketchel with Ralph Calloway. Stanley's poor performance against Klaus caused the promoters to take that action. There is some talk here that Ketchel held back in the fight and did not hit when the blow seemed dangerous. Hugo Kelly may meet Klaus here in Pittsburgh. Stan needed rest and would travel alone to Michigan and stay with his folks a few weeks before he gets ready to start his training at his camp. He would send a wire to the team and Wilson Mizner when he's ready. Ketchel's next battle will be the most controversial and mysterious of his magnificent career. His classic six round battle with the great immortal Sam Langford now awaits.

Ketchel's battle with Langford would take place on April 27, 1910, in the small National Athletic Club in Philadelphia, with Ketchel conceding 19 pounds to his opponent. Ketchel arrived in Philadelphia with his team on the evening of April 26 and spent the night in a luxurious hotel not far from the Athletic Club. The next morning, Ketchel tipped the beam at a solid 159 pounds. He seemed to be his championship self again. He was fiery in action and, for the first time in a long time, he had a fabulous physique. But the "Boston Tar Baby", as Langford was called, was no less fit, weighing in at a solid 178 pounds while standing only 5'7". Ketchel had been fighting since 1903, while Langford had only gone into the ring in search of a living the previous year. But By 1910, Langford seemed to have met them all: Jim Flynn, Joe Jennette, Mike Schereck, Tony Ross, Jim Berry, Larry Temple and Sandy Ferguson, and he had knocked out Iron Huge in four rounds in London, England, the previous year.

Ketchel's fight with Langford was set in Philadelphia because of the tremendous wave of publicity that Ketchel was riding. The fight was to be a prelude to a mega rematch between Ketchel and Langford that would take place in San Francisco and last 45 rounds. Jimmy Coffroth stood ready to put up $30,000 for the fight and let the fighters split it any way they liked.

"I know nothing about a fight in California, and after I get finished with Ketchel in Philly, there won't be any demand for another fight." Langford announced.

Nevertheless, Ketchel and Langford were indeed supposed to "tune up" in Philadelphia and then set sail for the "Golden West" and a bigger payday. Ketchel's fight with Langford in Philadelphia drew in a little over $18,750 and set a record for the Quaker city. Ketchel had been offered 50 percent of the gross, while Langford, of course, took less. In Ketchel's era, black fighters had to make financial concessions or receive no pay at all. Ultimately, Langford would collect $5,000.

In the opening round the fighters were cautious, stalking and pecking but not fighting, and the second round was the same. By the end of the second, the fans were hissing and booing, and then began cursing, spitting and throwing cigar butts into the ring. Ketchel became irritated by the attitude of the onlookers.

"What the hell they yelling at me for!" screamed Ketchel at the end of the second round.

"Take it easy, boy," said Mizner, as he rubbed Ketchel's neck. "Don't blow your top. Let them yell all they want, ignore it. Just concentrate on our $30,000. Please kid, please try to hold- back, please!"

But it was too late. Ketchel jumped from his stool and opened the third with a maniacal rush, crashing a terrific right to Langford's jaw and following it with a right to the body. Langford immediately came back with a right swing to the chin. Ketchel was stunned but returned with a left-right-left combination to Langford's jaw. He forced Langford to the ropes and caught him with a straight right to the cheekbone. They continued to mix it up and, just before the bell, Ketchel introduced Langford to the Ketchel shift. Langford was wobbly, but he recovered to smash Ketchel on the face with a right.

In Round four, Langford rushed Ketchel against the ropes, hitting him with two lefts to the midsection. Then they went into a clinch, but Langford worked his way out and ripped into Ketchel's body, then delivered a jab to the face and a hook to the head followed by a straight right. Ketchel was bleeding profusely form his nose but was fighting back with all his might. He shot a mighty right to the jaw but it missed. Had it landed, Langford might have been floored. But as it was, Langford ducked and caught the blow on the ear. The skin was instantly sliced and blood began to flow. At the end of the round, it was all Langford, and the fans began to think that Langford's weight advantage was too much for Ketchel, even in a six rounder.

Ketchel didn't sit on his stool between rounds, and burst out of his corner with a rush when the bell sounded. Langford, who had appeared dismal throughout the entire fight, now appeared even more dismal. He did every thing he knew to keep Ketchel away, but Ketchel kept tearing in. For a moment, Langford decided to stand up and fight it out with Ketchel. But he quickly decided otherwise and instead began using his "running shoes," hoping to tire Ketchel out. As the crowd hissed and booed at Langford, Ketchel remained in hot pursuit and, mysteriously, made Langford break into a smile. Near the end of the round, Langford stopped avoiding Ketchel and swung a right with everything he had. Had it reached its target, Ketchel would have dropped to the canvas. Langford swung so hard that he fell on his knees and elbows, feeling a little foolish and laughing at his own discomfiture.

"Who is Langford trying to kid?" sneered one reporter. "He couldn't miss that badly if he was drunk and had one leg cut off."

At the beginning of the sixth and final round, the fighters shook hands. Then Ketchel immediately went after Langford as he had done in the fifth. Langford started to run again, and the fans shouted and stomped until the rafters shook. As Ketchel kept charging, both men went to the ropes. But they were soon in the middle of the ring again, then on one side of the ring and soon the other. As before, Langford eventually stopped running and tried to stem the tide. But when he did land blows, Ketchel seemed to shake them off. As the round neared completion, Langford began to tire and no longer tried to escape Ketchel. Instead, he tried to clinch. But Ketchel tore himself loose and continued his berserk attack. When the final bell rang, Langford smiled with relief, and the crowd gave Ketchel a standing ovation. Ketchel walked over to Langford's corner and shook his hand one last time after the gloves were off. Langford whispered in Ketchel's ear: "See you in San Francisco, Stanley."

Because victory by decision was not permitted in Pennsylvania in 1910, there would be a variety of verdicts as to who won the fight. Some experts thought that Langford hadn't given his best to spare Ketchel from a knockout, while others gave the victory to Ketchel, or called the fight a draw. There were times in the fight when the action was slow and the fighters stalled. But once Ketchel was stung by Langford's heavy wallops, he took the fight more seriously. Ketchel's brilliant performance in the last two rounds gained him the admiration of the spectators and brought him the winner's verdict from the majority of the crowd. With the brief contest over, Langford declared that he had done his best, but that Ketchel's brutal style in the last two rounds proved too much for him.

Langford would later remark about Ketchel's fighting ability: "Ketchel's fighting technique is a sheer 'tumultuous ferocity', a rage that is barely controlled." As for Ketchel's rushes, Langford commented:

"I never saw any man coming at me like that before, I hope I never see it again."

After the fight, one reporter said that, "when the fifth round began, Stan became an animal. His eyes were so wild and large that he didn't look mean, but beyond that. It was the quickness of the change that startled me because you never see it coming."

In answering questions about Langford, Ketchel declared that he had tried for a knockout every minute of the fight and that, had Langford not spent the last two rounds running around the ring, he might have succeeded. Throughout his time as a professional fighter, Ketchel had a peculiar longing to see his opponents on the day following a fight. He made it a rule throughout his career to seek out the unhappy loser that he might console him and offer him a part of his purse. According to one story, following his battle with Langford, Ketchel shared a bottle of expensive champagne with Langford and gave him a wad of bills so large that Langford couldn't fit it in his pocket. According to one source, Langford received more money from Ketchel than he did from the boxing promoters. Ketchel's generosity to Langford was typical of his generosity toward everyone that he liked. But he probably also felt confident about spreading his wealth due to the big payday that he figured to share with Langford in San Francisco. Unfortunately, he would not live to see it.

Chapter 19:
Ketchel vs. Flynn, Lewis and Smith

In the spring of 1910, Ketchel made another trip to Michigan to bring his father east so he could attend his next three fights, the first of which would be against Porky Flynn. Flynn was born in Boston Massachusetts on April 5, 1888. He was muscular and well developed, and had earned the nickname Porky because of his love for pork scrapple. Some fighters claimed that Porky was the meanest fighter they ever faced. In his fight with Ketchel, that meanness would be put to the ultimate test. Ketchel's 20-round bout with Flynn took place on May 18, at Boston, Massachusetts' Armory Arena. The following is an account of the fight from a 1910 edition of the *Grand Rapids Herald*:

> Ketchel had a very successful title defense by putting a quick end to his fight with rugged Porky Flynn at the Armory A.A. of Boston. Though it was a short fight, it gave Ketchel and Flynn fans a chance to see why the "Michigan Assassin" was rated a great middleweight. "When going at full speed, he was wonderful to see" said an eyewitness. Three rounds

were sufficient for Ketchel to put Porky away. The third round had hardly started when Flynn crashed face first from Ketchel's tricky shift and he remained down for a count of nine. He was wobbly when he got to his feet but was able to deliver a weak blow to Ketchel's stomach as the champion tore in for the kill. Ketchel showed no mercy. He fought at a very cruel pace and forced Flynn to the ropes and planted a left jab, straight right-left hook combination to the jaw, at the same time ripping a left to the body. And Porky Flynn a top middleweight contender fell to the canvas in a heartbeat. He never twitched a muscle as he was counted out. It was a slaughter so far as Porky was concerned. From a mild tempered, quiet young man before the fight, Ketchel transformed to a fighting whirlwind intent only on Flynn's destruction. He tore and ripped in from beginning to end with absolutely no letting up. Stanley was never a believer in stopping. The more punches he absorbed the more destructive he became. He wasted no time on hurling himself on his opponent with fists flying from all directions. Willie Lewis will be Ketchel's next battle.

Ketchel's May 27th fight with Willie Lewis was one of the most sensational short bouts ever staged in New York's National Athletic Club. Before the second round was halfway through, the bout ended. Ketchel's right glove caught Lewis squarely on the point of the jaw in the midst of a heated exchange and flattened him. Throughout the short fight, Ketchel boxed uncharacteristically cautiously, following his opponent around the ring and never making an unnecessary move. He shot his punches on target with all the force he could muster. Lewis retreated in a hurry before Ketchel's advances and, whenever the opportunity presented itself, lashed out with rights and lefts that landed hard. But the end arrived so fast that only the people at ringside saw what happened. The following is an account of Ketchel's bout with Lewis from a 1910 edition of the *Grad Rapids Herald*:

Stanley Ketchel, the middleweight champion of the world, knocked out Willie Lewis of this city in the second round of a scheduled 10 round at the National Sporting Club tonight. Lewis who was the Parisian idol some months ago, is a welterweight and was full 10 pounds lighter than Ketchel, who weighed in this afternoon at a solid 158 pounds, according to agreement. Tom O'Rourke then manager of the club, acted as referee. The crowd numbered about 8,000. Lewis with green trunks went right at his man in the opening round with showing any sign of fear. They exchanged body blows at close quarters, with Ketchel having the better of the exchanges. Lewis stepped cleverly inside of a vicious right hand and planted a straight left on Stanley's face a moment later. After another session of in fighting Ketchel with red trunks sent a crisp left hook to the face and the bell ended the round. Lewis was extremely confident when he stepped into the center of the ring in the second round. He went at Ketchel furiously, but the fast pace really suited Ketchel who, after a few exchanges, planted a hard left on Lewis's body followed with a terrific left hook on the jaw. Lewis was out before he hit the canvas and fell face first and was counted out. He lay there motionless for several minutes before helping him out of the ring. Ketchel retained his middleweight championship.

After Ketchel knocked out Lewis, Lewis's manager, Dan Mcketrick, approached him. Mcketrick knew that Ketchel had been convinced to change managers once before, and he decided to try to convince him once more. Mcketrick found Ketchel receptive to the idea and called Mizner to apprise him of the deal.

"That's fine," Mizner said. "It will be quite a relief to me. Did Ketchel tell you that I owe him $3,000?"

Mcketrick was a little surprised, and he knew that the only way that Ketchel could collect the debt was to stay under Mizner's management. Mcketrick hurried to Ketchel's dressing room for verification.

"Does Wilson owe you $3,000?" asked Mcketrick.

Ketchel turned white and strode the floor.

"Well how about it?" demanded Mcketrick.

Ketchel turned whiter and kept striding. Then he acknowledged the debt. He would be Mizner's fighter until Mizner could pay, which, based on Mizner's past form, might be never.

A few days later, Willie Lewis, his jaw swollen like a melon, sat dismally in his nightgown, in his East side New York apartment. He looked out the window and saw Ketchel pull up to the curb in his red roadster. Lewis winced. Ketchel was the last person he wanted to see. But Ketchel had leapt form his car and was heading into the building. Soon, Lewis heard knocking at his door. When he answered the door, Ketchel replied, "Get your pants on, we're gonna blow this town wide open."

Lewis wanted to stay home and put ice on his aching face, but it was useless to argue. When he returned home two days later, he wasn't sure of all the places that Ketchel had dragged him to, but he had had an incredible time, and his swelling was gone. While Ketchel was out on his all night party adventures in New York's most glamorous dance halls, Thomas Ketchel would stay in one of the most beautiful hotel suites New York had to offer. He was having a wonderful trip. The next day he and Stanley bought dozens of gifts to bring back to the Ketchel residence and enjoyed the sights of New York City. Ketchel's next bout would be against Jim Smith at the National Sporting Club on June 11th.

Ketchel found Smith to be a tough opponent, but only for a while. Smith, by his aggressive determination, had just begun to get the crowd on his side when he received a fatal blow. He had beaten Ketchel on points in the first round, taking advantage of Ketchel's open defense as he drove him about the ring with right and left swings to the body and head. In the fourth round, after taking a beating, Smith came back with a vicious attack and stunned Ketchel from head to heels, sending him staggering toward his corner from a smashing right to the jaw. Smith's determination did not fail him even when he was sent to the canvas. He wanted the title badly, and he made four desperate efforts to get to his feet. But his body could stand no more and he collapsed to the floor, where he remained until helped by his seconds to his corner.

Ketchel received a standing ovation from the 8,000 spectators and waved for several minutes. Then he climbed out of the ring and went ringside to hug his father. The fans started to chant Ketchel's name as he walked down the aisle to leave the arena and travel to Grand Rapids. It would be Ketchel's last time in a boxing arena.

Ketchel arrived at the Grand Rapids train station on Thursday Sept 1, 1910, and rented a cab for the next nine miles to Detroit. His family was happy to see him and he promised that he would stay for his 23rd birthday on the 14th. He settled down and prepared for an extended rest. The following week, Ketchel, his father and his brothers spent time horseback riding, hunting, fishing, swimming and viewing new films at the local theater. Ketchel and his mother spent happy times together as well, dining in fancy restaurants and buying jewelry and expensive clothing. Ketchel visited the catholic school in Grand Rapids that he once attended and surprised the children and nuns with cake and ice cream. Ketchel held them spellbound as he told stories of his exciting and dangerous life. It was a special moment that the students would never forget.

On Monday, Sept 12, R.P. Dickerson stopped by the Ketchel residence in a limousine. He wanted to see his childhood friend, Julia, and her champion son. Ketchel told Dickerson that he was going to stay in Michigan and buy his own spread close to his parents. But Dickerson ended up convincing him that his health would recoup faster if he stayed at his ranch in Missouri. At first, Ketchel was skeptical about the idea. But the more Dickerson talked the more he wanted to go. Dickerson telegraphed his ranch that, on Sept 15, he would be returning on the evening train with Ketchel. Dickerson loved Ketchel like a son, and Ketchel instantly fell in love with Dickerson's Ozark ranch. But the love affair would be short lived. Four weeks later, a young couple would arrive in Springfield in search of work and altar the course of Ketchel's life.

Chapter 20:
Walter and Goldie

Walter Sylvester Dipley was born in Christian County, Missouri, on April 8, 1887. He was the last of five children. His father, Walter Scott Dipley, was a local Baptist preacher at the Oak Grove Church, and would eventually help form the White River Baptist Association. Dipley senior and his wife, Mary Maxwell, raised their children in a log cabin, later moving to Webb City where they owned a plot of land. The Dipley children grew up to be hard working citizens, although Walter displayed a violent temper that continually caused trouble. On February 26, 1908, Walter Dipley enlisted in the Navy, only to be discharged on September 24, 1909, for intoxication and fighting with other navy men aboard ship. Dipley was court-martialed twice during his stint with the Navy—once being sentenced to 10 to 20 days solitary confinement—and his highest rank was Ordinary Seaman. In early 1910, he returned to Webb City, drifted from job to job, and started hitting the bottle.

Goldie Smith was born in 1888 in Texas County. She married in 1903 at the age of 13 and married again a year later. Her second marriage produced a child. But the Texas County court removed the child due to Goldie's "moral character and the bad life she was leading." In 1908, at age 18, Goldie married yet again, this time in Kansas. But, as before, the marriage would be short lived.

In August and September of 1908, Dipley was visiting his parents in Webb City. On September 11th, he departed Webb City to visit his older sister, Nancy, in Blue Creek. After leaving Blue Creek, Dipley returned to Springfield, borrowing money from his father to get a ride on the Chadwick Flyer. On the same train was Goldie Smith. She was on her way home from Kansas to stay with her mother and stepfather, who lived in the same neighborhood as Dipley's sister. Chadwick was as far the train tracks went; and after dropping it's load of passengers and freight, the locomotive swung around in a turntable and headed back to Springfield. Goldie went to a cheap hotel and asked its constable and manager, John Boles, how she could get to her mother's home that was located 10 miles south. Boles told her that, "a young fellow here is going out to the same community. It might make it cheaper on both of you to hire a carriage together and go out." The young man was Walter Dipley.

Goldie and Walter met in the hotel lobby, hired a carriage, and started south to their different destinations. They were attracted to each other instantly, and Walter presented an idea: they should tell his sister that they had recently married so that they could stay together at her house. Goldie immediately agreed, and when they arrived in Blue Creek, Walter introduced her as his lovely wife. Later that night, the couple walked out to the barn to look at the stock, and Dipley decided to make their fake marriage a legitimate one. Goldie refused, saying that she was in no condition to marry a fourth time, as she didn't know if she was divorced from her former husband, and was not living the right kind of life. However, she agreed that they should live together as man and wife and get married as soon she found out if she were free to get a divorce.

On Sunday, September 18, Walter and Goldie visited Goldie's relatives and stayed for three weeks. Upon leaving, they headed to Springfield to look for jobs, checking in at a cheap hotel under the last name, Hurtz. Three days later, Walter walked a few blocks to Spear's employment office at 321½ College Street to ask for jobs for himself and Goldie.

"I don't think I have any jobs for you, Mr. Dipley. I'm sorry about that," said Mr. Spear.

After a brief conversation, Dipley thanked him and turned to walk out the door. Then Mr. Spear called his name.

"You know what, I just thought of something. I might have a job for you. Is your wife a stout and healthy woman?"

"Yes, she is," replied Dipley.

With that, Spear sent them to see R.P. Dickerson. They would arrive at his ranch at 3 p.m. sharp.

"This man is very particular," Spear told Dipley, "and he wants to see a party before he hires them. He just got back from Grand Rapids on vacation. You made it just in time."

Dickerson's veteran Ranch hand, C.E. Bailey, would soon be dismissed and replaced by Ketchel. Ketchel was inexperienced in ranching as well as business, so Dickerson went to Spear's employment office to find a hard working ranch hand and housekeeper to help him. When Spear's described Walter and Goldie, Dickerson was satisfied.

"What is their last name," Dickerson asked, and was given the name, Hurtz.

After interviewing Walter and Goldie, Dickerson hired them on the spot as ranch hand and housekeeper, respectively.

"Your wages will be $30 a month, along with room and board. I'm going to my Ozark ranch on Wednesday morning," Dickerson told them. "I'm going to make a change out there. Both of you can go to work right away then and meet your new boss while I'm away on a business trip. His name his Stanley Ketchel."

On the morning of October 12th, Walter and Goldie met Dickerson at the Springfield train depot and boarded the Pullman for Conway, which held the closest railroad station to Dickerson's spread. It wasn't until they got off the train at Conway in the late afternoon that Dickerson introduced them to Stanley Ketchel, whom he had spent the entire train ride with in the smoking car. It was the first time that Walter and Goldie had heard the name Stanley Ketchel, and they studied him closely. What was going through their minds at that moment is a mystery. But it is certain that, when they found out that Ketchel was the famous Michigan Assassin, they began contemplating his wealth. After exiting the train, the four of them went across the street to a livery stable and Dickerson bought a carriage ride to the ranch. When they arrived at the ranch, Goldie and Walter were placed in a log cabin that was separated from the main house by a hollow. In two days, they would settle into the main house to assist Ketchel. Early the next morning, Dickerson went back to Conway and returned to Springfield for his business trip, accompanied by his wife and her hired girl.

On his first day at the ranch, Dipley was busy working in the fields and painting the north side of a new barn, while Goldie cooked Ketchel's meals in the main house. That night, after supper, Walter borrowed a .22 Caliber rifle from Ketchel, telling him that he needed it to kill varmints. Ketchel also had a Colt .45 revolver, which he carried conspicuously in his waistband and practiced with daily. On the morning of Friday the 14th, Ketchel was target practicing and Dipley was nearby, painting the rest of the barn. Suddenly, Dipley approached him, inquiring about Ketchel's motives with the gun. According to one account, Ketchel responded to Dipley's inquiry by mentioning an attempt on his life that had taken place in New York. "I want to be a good revolver shot," Ketchel had added.

The next morning, Ketchel awoke at 5 a.m. for his usual early morning jog. Returning to the main house, he found Goldie preparing his breakfast. He washed up and sat down to eat. He was suspicious as to why a single chair was placed at the table with its back to the outside door. But he decided to sit down and Goldie served him his meal. After Ketchel sat down, the door behind him slowly crept open. Walter Dipley stepped inside and crept up behind Ketchel with Ketchel's rifle. He aimed at Ketchel's back and fired. Ketchel dropped his utensils, raised his hand to his chest and slumped to the floor. Then he struggled to his feet and started staggering, eventually gaining his equilibrium. But just as he gained his balance, he fell again. Ketchel tried to draw his revolver. But Dipley leaned over and seized it. After a brief struggle, Dipley overpowered Ketchel and smashed his face with the butt of the revolver. With Ketchel down, Walter and Goldie stole rolls of bills from his wallet and removed his diamond ring.

At the time of the shooting, C.E. Bailey and Luther Brazeale had been in the pasture, looking for cows that had wondered off during the night. Between 6:30 and 7:00 a.m., they returned to see Walter and Goldie coming out of the main house, with Dipley carrying Ketchel's revolver.

"What's going on? What's the trouble?" Bailey asked.

"I shot the…"

Walter didn't go any further. Bailey became suspicious and headed to the main house. As he entered the kitchen, he heard a faint cry and saw a blood trail that led to Ketchel's bedroom. When Bailey entered the bedroom, he stood aghast. A pool of blood spread out from

Ketchel's bed, where he was moaning and coughing up blood, his hand tightly clenching his chest. Bailey knelt down to observe Ketchel and discovered few signs of life. He held Ketchel's hand and asked loudly, "Stanley, speak to me. How did this happen? Wake up!"

Ketchel moved his head and his eyes fluttered open. Ketchel gazed at Bailey but didn't seem to recognize him. As he tried to speak, Bailey put his ear to his mouth.

"They shot me," Ketchel whispered.

"Who, who shot you?" Bailey implored. "Please tell me!"

Ketchel tried to raise his head and used the last of his strength to speak.

"I was sitting at the kitchen table, and I was shot in the back by this man Hurtz. Get the woman too, for she robbed me."

Bailey knew exactly whom Ketchel was talking about, and he told him to hang on while he got help. Bailey left the bedroom, went to the kitchen's back door and yelled at several ranch hands that were working in the barn.

"Luther, Jim, George!" Bailey screamed at the top of his lungs. "Hitch up the fastest team, drive to Conway. Then telephone Mr. Dickerson at Springfield. Tell him Mr. Ketchel's been shot. Tell him to bring the best doctors and hurry here!"

Jim ran to a carriage and hitched Colonel Dickerson's fastest pair of black horses to a light rig and raced toward Conway across the rutty, bumpy roads. Bailey went to his friend Brazeale's house and found Dipley and Goldie there. He advised Walter to surrender to the town constable, Alex Anderson, who lived close by. But Walter had other plans. He left Goldie at Brazeale's and made his escape through the woods after Bailey went back to the house to look in on Ketchel. Dipley started south toward the railroad tracks and the main road to

Niangua. Later, the police would ask him why he hadn't surrendered to the Constable.

"Well, I was in a little fear; I didn't know what might have happened if I give up there to him. I knew Marshfield was the county seat, and I thought I would come over here and give up to the sheriff," Dipley explained.

Meanwhile, George telephoned Dickerson in Springfield to give him the terrible news. Dickerson called two of Springfield's best physicians, Dr. Fulbright and Dr. Fulton, as well as Emmett Newton, a good friend and newspaper man, and Springfield policeman, Alfred Sampey, to accompany him. Dickerson also wired the police in New York to bring bloodhounds, police officers and five nurses to Missouri. Dickerson called on all the help his wealth could command in order to save Ketchel's life and catch Dipley. Four states, Missouri, California, New York, and Illinois were about to begin the biggest manhunt ever witnessed in Webster County. Within the hour, Dickerson's train raced toward Conway, with Dickerson pacing back and forth and calling for more speed. The train was approaching Strafford when Dickerson realized that no one had called the Webster County sheriff, C.B. "Cobe" Shields, to tell him the tragic news. Shields would be the key investigator in the case.

The train reached the Conway train station at 11 a.m., where four carriages were waiting. Dickerson, Dr. Newton, Dr. Fulbright, Cobe Shields, two reporters and several deputies quickly piled into them. They made the five-mile trip from Conway to the ranch in 35 minutes, arriving at 11:45 a.m. By this time, a large crowd had started to gather at the ranch, and Dr. O.C. Benage from Conway had been helping Ketchel for some time. Dickerson jumped out of the carriage before it made a full stop, running for the main house as fast his legs could carry him. He was the first of the new arrivals to enter Ketchel's room. When he entered, he stood in shock, unable to recognize Ketchel because of the blood and wounds that covered his face. Dickerson walked to Ketchel's bed and quietly conversed with Dr. Benage. But they were only able to get a few words out before the room flooded with doctors and nurses.

Dickerson retreated to the dining room while the three doctors began their attempt to pull the bullet from Ketchel's back. Dickerson conferred with Bailey and Bailey related what he saw.

"I saw Ketchel shot, brutally beaten on the face. Stanley had a .45 Colt revolver under his shirt, tucked it into his belt at all times. When I found him with his shirt pulled out, the blue-gun was gone because Walter had it. Hurtz approached me last night and said he was quitting the job because he didn't want to cause trouble, and I asked what was the trouble. But he refused to give me any details. Since I was leaving the ranch the next morning, he wanted to come with me and I told him yes he could come along. But more than anything else, he and Goldie were acting very strangely."

Dickerson balled up his fists and started accusing Dipley of killing his "son". Then he stormed out of the house and made a magnificent offer to the gathering crowd and every resident in Webster County. "Post a reward for $5,000", he exclaimed. "The reward would be paid for Hurtz dead, and not one cent for him alive!"

A half hour later, the physicians exited Ketchel's bedroom. Dr. Fulbright went over to Dickerson to give him the news.

"Rollin, I'm sorry. We cannot find the bullet. His condition is very critical. Mr. Ketchel has lost too much blood. The bullet struck a major blood vessel in his right lung and the pleural cavity is filling with blood, making breathing difficult for him. Ever since I've been here, he's been asking for water because he is thirsty."

"What is it you want to say doctor? Spill it out," Dickerson said crisply.

"What I'm trying to say is that Mr. Ketchel is slowly suffocating. Pretty soon he won't be able to breath at all. Our only hope is to get him to the Springfield Hospital. We have facilities there for an operation that will hopefully save his life."

Dickerson looked at the doctor with a hard stare. He knew it was a grave risk taking a wounded man on a long journey back to Conway over bumpy roads.

"All right," Dickerson said. "We'll do it if you say it's best."

Dickerson went back outside and delivered a heartfelt command to find Dipley, who was still known as Walter Hurtz. "I hope he isn't arrested alive. I'm willing to give $5,000 to the man who kills him. He deserves nothing better. You men get on your horses and hunt him down. Down be afraid to shoot him. He is armed and won't hesitate to shoot you. He showed that when he shot Stanley Ketchel in the back. Hurtz might try to get a train somewhere here and one of you may get him. Be on the lookout!"

Dr. Fulbright gave Dickerson Ketchel's remaining rings. The limp body of what had been one of the most incredible boxers in history was carried on a stretcher to a spring wagon that was waiting beside the ranch house. Because the journey was made slowly to avoid a bumpy ride, two and a half hours had elapsed by the time they arrived at the Conway train station, where they encountered a long delay. A mob began gathering, trying to catch a glimpse of Ketchel as he lay on a stretcher inside the wagon. Dickerson repeated his reward to the mob.

"Shoot first, then yell halt," Dickerson screamed. "I have enough money to protect anyone who kills Hurtz. I want his head or arm to hang on my living room wall." As news of the large reward spread across the countryside, residents gathered their traps, shotguns, horses and dogs to begin the search for Missouri's biggest fugitive.

Finally, the locomotive rumbled into Conway and made a screeching halt as it stopped at the depot. After it departed for Springfield, Dickerson ordered the train's engineer to blow warning signals until they reach their destination. Over the years, versions of where Ketchel spoke his last words before he lapsed to unconsciousness have stated that he spoke them at the ranch, on the way to the hospital or in the hospital. But he probably spoke them inside the ranch house. By the time he reached the train and the hospital, he had lost so much blood that he couldn't speak. According to C. E. Bailey's description: "Stanley opened his eyes and gazed at the ceiling and had a faint smile on his face. Like a little child, he whispered: 'I'm so tired…take me home to mother', and closed his eyes peacefully."

Back at the ranch, Sheriff Shields started questioning the ranch hands and developed some interesting information. No one had seen Dipley approach the main house on the morning of the crime. But the evening before, several eyewitnesses had seen Ketchel talking with Dipley near the new barn. They had had an argument that was filled with foul language. Shields had several questions racing across his mind. But the thing that caught his attention the most was the fact that Dipley had arrived at the ranch with Goldie. Shields heard from other workers that Dipley and Goldie were married, and that Dipley had a vicious temper. It was reported that Dipley told Goldie two days before the shooting: "I'll kill any man who looks at you twice."

Shields had a feeling that Goldie was an accomplice to Ketchel's murder and decided to question her. One important question needed to be answered: Why did Goldie only place one chair at the table facing away from the kitchen door? By this time, the news of Ketchel's shooting was on the front pages of newspapers across the U.S. The following is an article from the *Grand Rapids Herald* on October 15, 1910:

Stanley Ketchel, champion middleweight pugilist, was shot and it is believed, fatally wounded, five miles North of Conway, Mo. near here this morning. Ketchel left the city several weeks ago accompanied by his friend Rollin Dickerson. He was determined to take a long rest and endeavor to recuperate so he might defend, the championship against the many challengers and fight. Reporters have reached his relatives in this city recently in the effect that the champion had purchased a large farm in the vicinity in Springfield Mo. and had settled down on the ranch. Convinced that he would not be able to again do himself justice in the ring. The champion was born in Grand Rapids Michigan, September 14th, 1887 and therefore was twenty-three years of age last month. He left his home city at the age of twelve to seek fame and fortune for his folks and journeying by easy stages until he reached Butte. Mont, where he secured employment in the mines, he worked as a bellhop in the Copper Queen Casino and various other kinds of work in Butte before taking pugilism as a profession.

When the Ketchel family received the shocking news, his parents wept bitterly. Julia wanted to head for Springfield to be with her son. She told Thomas and her four sons that she would go alone if she could. Dickerson sent an urgent telegram to the Ketchel's Family and pleaded with them to stay home, saying that they wouldn't have enough patience for the long trip. Ketchel's brothers, John and Leon, agreed with Dickerson and convinced their mother to stay home. But they didn't want the courier to go through the trouble of traveling nine miles back and forth to send more telegrams of Ketchel's condition, so they took a carriage to Grand Rapids to stay at the wire and telegram office to await further news. When Hype Igoe received the awful news in New York, he hurried to the luxurious Bartholdi Hotel and interrupted Wilson Mizner's card game. Tears were pouring down his face as he told Wilson what had happened.

"Stanley's going to die," Hype said.

"No he ain't," Mizner chuckled.

"But he's got a bullet in his lung," Hype replied.

"It doesn't matter," Mizner said with a laugh. "Just tell them to start counting. Before they get to ten, Stan will get up!"

Back at the ranch, Goldie was being watched by Marshfield police officers in the dining room. Sheriff Shields was ready to question her, and called her to the front porch. Goldie's eyes shifted uneasily as she waited to be questioned. Otherwise, she betrayed no emotion.

"Did you set the chair in front of the Kitchen backdoor? I mean directly in front of the screened door?" Shields asked her

"Yes, I suppose I did. Maybe Mr. Ketchel moved it. I can't recall."

"What do you mean you suppose?" Shields asked. Then he shifted his line of questioning abruptly. "You heard the shot that struck Ketchel?"

"Yes, I heard it."

"Yet you didn't go to Mr. Ketchel to help him or call for help."

After hesitating, Goldie replied, "No, I was too frightened to move."

"And you didn't see Hurtz with the gun?" Shields continued.

"No," Goldie replied.

"And you didn't see or hear Hurtz enter the house and approach Ketchel from behind?"

"No," she answered again.

Goldie stared at the porch floor as she answered, but then she raised her eyes.

"I first saw Mr. Ketchel this morning when he came from his bedroom dressed for breakfast. I had heard him doing his exercises, and I already had the table ready for his breakfast. I had started to cook his ham and eggs, too, when he stepped into the kitchen. I brought him his breakfast and returned to my place by the stove. A few minutes later, I heard angry voices, but I didn't recognize them. Then I heard a shot but I was too frightened to move. I saw no one, and a moment later, Mr. Bailey entered the kitchen and rushed into the dining room."

As Shields stared hard at Goldie, he couldn't shake the feeling that she was hiding something. He then left the porch and asked C.E. Bailey for his opinion of Goldie's answers.

"I don't believe her," Bailey snapped. "I recall Stanley telling her he didn't like his back facing the door when we helped him get settled in the main house. Somehow, Walter and Goldie premeditated all this. Hurtz was jealous of Ketchel; it was fairly obvious."

Soon, new discoveries would remove any doubt that Goldie knew more about the crime than she was revealing. First, a suitcase that belonged to Dipley was opened and a photograph was found that showed Walter and Goldie together, while another photograph showed a uniformed Dipley during his Navy days. On the back of one of the photos was written the name Walter Dipley, indicating that Hurtz was an alias. Shields immediately switched the $5,000 offer for Walter Hurtz to an offer for Walter Dipley. Throughout the Ozark Mountains, bloodhounds were barking and baying as they searched for Dipley's scent, and hundreds of armed cowboys were threading their way through steep hills and gullies. But the light was beginning to fade, and the search seemed to be going nowhere. At the ranch, Goldie sat under heavy guard in the dining room with an expressionless face. Shields ordered the deputies to send her to jail in nearby Marshfield for more questioning.

At the hospital, Dickerson stood at the foot of Ketchel's bed, staring at the pale face that lay silently on the pillow. Eventually, the staff gave Dickerson the unfortunate word that they had done all they could for Ketchel. The bullet was never located and Ketchel lapsed into a coma.

After 13 hours of clinging to life, Ketchel's suffering was coming to a close. At 7:01 p.m., Stanley Ketchel was pronounced dead. As soon as they received word of his death, Ketchel's brothers returned home to tell their parents. The Ketchel's were instantly grief stricken, and Julia was unable to speak. A short time later, John and Leon were notified that they could pick up Stanley's body at Ely Paxton's funeral home. Paxton would prepare Ketchel for burial and put a sign on the door that read: "Please wipe your feet before coming in to see the dead man." No autopsy was performed, and Paxton would do a decent job of covering the deep bruises on Ketchel's face.

Meanwhile, at the Marshfield jail, Sheriff Shields was putting increased pressure on Goldie after hours of interrogation, and her story started to change. She admitted that she was an eyewitness to the murder and that her common law husband's last name was Dipley, and that Dipley had shot Ketchel because he insulted her the day before the shooting:

> While I was working in the house yesterday, Ketchel insulted me. I became angry. He was greatly wrought up over the incident and pleaded with me not to say anything to Walter about our conversation. He said he would give me the best team of horses on the farm if I would keep quiet. I made him no promise. When Walter came home from the fields, I told him what Ketchel said to me. He was very angry. I think that is what made him kill Ketchel.

Goldie's theory on Dipley's motives brought many denials from the Dickerson ranch hands. The workers declared that Ketchel had not insulted Goldie, and that he had not been at the ranch when she said the incident occurred. Furthermore, they declared that Ketchel was a peacemaker at the ranch and had reprimanded Dipley the evening before the attack when he saw him beating one of Dickerson's horses.

Shields ultimately determined that Goldie's accusations weren't strong enough, and that she and Dipley had premeditated to take Ketchel's life. Goldie was charged as an accomplice to murder. But Walter Dipley was still nowhere to be found.

Chapter 21:
October 16, 1910 - The Capture

R.P. Dickerson was raving mad that Dipley was still on the loose, and he repeated his reward for Dipley's death over and over again. The special trains from California and New York hadn't arrived yet. But reinforcements from Illinois had already joined in the search. At 11:30 p.m., Dipley made his way through the mountain trails carrying Ketchel's pistol. He was journeying toward the small town of Marshfield, sometimes walking along railroad tracks and other times along Ozark creeks. When he was five miles from Marshfield, Dipley sat down to rest. Suddenly, he saw a light ahead; he couldn't tell if it was a house light or a lantern. As he questioned whether he should turn aside or continue along the dirt trail, he decided to investigate the light, which turned out to be house light. Nevertheless, Dipley was spooked, and from then on, he would stop at five-minute intervals, draw the gun, and listen for sounds of pursuit. As Dipley skulked along the trail toward the house, his legs felt like jelly and his face was streaked with dirt. He knew that approaching the house would be risky, but his weariness made the risk seem worthwhile.

When he arrived on the house's property, he hid Ketchel's pistol in a log corncrib. Then he knocked at the front door. Thomas Hoggard, who occupied the house with his children, heard Dipley's knock as he was getting ready for bed. When he opened the front door, he saw a young man whose clothes and face were briar torn.

"I'm lost," Dipley whispered. "I'm from Christian County. I was hunting stray horses, two bay mares with a star on the forehead, and I lost my way. I've been walking all day and have had nothing to eat. If you'll give me something to eat and a place to sleep, I'll pay for it in the morning."

"Come in," Hoggard said. "I can take care of you, but I don't want your money. Sit down over here by the fire." Dipley asked to use the telephone and called for information about Goldie. Hoggard overheard him asking about the whereabouts of the "wife of the man who done the shooting." After supper, Dipley was told he could sleep in an upstairs room, and he went to bed. Hoggard sent his children to ask his neighbor, C.Z. "Zib" Murphy, for his opinion on Dipley's presence. Murphy had heard about Ketchel's shooting over the telephone and suspected that Hoggard's sudden houseguest might be the man. Murphy returned with Hoggard's children, but he and Hoggard couldn't decide if Dipley was the culprit. They tried to call the Marshfield police for Dipley's description but were unable to get through. As a result, Murphy spent the night shuttling back and forth through the neighborhood, making phone calls in an attempt to get Dipley's description. Murphy returned to the Hoggard's farm at about 4 a.m., finding him still awake. Because Hoggard had run out of oil for his lamps, they sat together in the dark.

At about 6:30 a.m., Hoggard's brother, Joe, appeared at the farm to request his brother's help in burying a mare that had died on his farm. Joe had been in Wright County the previous day and had heard about the shooting soon after it happened. But he wasn't able to remember a clear description of the perpetrator. All he knew for certain was that the wanted fugitive had a tattoo of "Hong Kong China" on his forearm. For Joe's brother and Murphy, the information was a godsend, and they decided to look in on Dipley to see if he had the critical mark. When they entered Dipley's bedroom, he was sitting on the bed. Murphy and Thomas demanded to see his arms, and Dipley obliged. At the sight of the tattoo, Hoggard and Murphy told Dipley to consider himself under arrest. After discovering Ketchel's diamond ring and money in Dipley's pockets, the Hoggard brothers and Murphy left with Dipley for Marshfield, walking a mile and a half to Niangua to get a carriage.

On the way, Dipley told Joe, "I'm the duck they are looking for. I shot Ketchel in self-defense. I didn't mean to shoot him. I aimed to arrest him and take him to Conway for insulting my wife."

As they waited for their carriage in Niangua, Joe bought Dipley breakfast at a hotel. Then just before they left, they received a telephone call from Thomas' house telling them that a gun had been found in the corncrib. On the way to Marshfield, they stopped by Thomas' house and picked it up. The group arrived in Marshfield at about 10 a.m. But the sheriff wasn't in town.

"I wouldn't deliver him until I saw shields," Joe said later." I said I wanted a receipt for him until the sheriff came back. I turned him in there and the gun and got a receipt for it."

The following is an article from the October 17th edition of the *Marshfield Chronicle* announcing Dipley's capture:

> Walter Dipley, Alias Walter Hurtz, shot and killed Stanley Ketchel, the middleweight champion prizefighter of the world, at the R.P. Dickerson ranch in Union township,

Saturday morning of last week at about 6:30 while Ketchel was sitting at the table eating his breakfast, the weapon used being a twenty –two caliber Marlin rifle. The bullet entered Ketchel's body at the back just below the right shoulder and lodged in the right lung, producing a wound that caused the champion's death about 7o'clock that evening. Dipley, who was an entire stranger, was sent to the ranch, from Springfield by R.P. Dickerson, the owner of the ranch, only a few days before to work on the farm, at the time going by the name of Hurtz. As soon as news of the shooting reached Springfield Dickerson chartered a special train to take him, doctors, officers, nurses and bloodhounds to the scene of the crime. Soon after the shooting Dipley, after securing Ketchel's revolver, a big 45 –Colt, struck out through the woods to make his escape. Although there were several of the employees of the ranch near when the shooting took place, none of them attempted to capture Dipley as none of them was armed, and he walked leisurely away. After wandering through the woods all day to avoid capture. Dipley appeared at the farm home of Thos. Hoggard, a mile or so out of Niangua, between 9 and 10 o'clock Saturday night and asked permission to stay all night, remarking that he was hunting his horses and had became lost, and permission being given he soon retired. Soon after the stranger retired Mr. Hoggard became suspicious that he might be the man who the officers were searching for and communicated his suspicions to Zib Murphy, a neighbor, and the two watched the house to guard against the stranger's leaving. Joe Hoggard a brother happened along about daylight Sunday morning when the three men went to Dipley's room and placed him under arrest. When they entered the room occupied by Dipley they found him setting on the side of the bed with his head in his hands. After they had placed him under arrest and searched him for weapons they made him roll up his sleeves in search of the tattoo marks that was known to be on the arms of the slayer, and finding them, knew they had the right man. When searched they found dollar bills, a ring and a small pocket knife, the prisoner telling his captors that he hid the revolver he had taken from Ketchel's body, in the corn crib by the barn before approaching the house the night before. The prisoner was taken to Niangua where a conveyance was procured and he was brought to this place and lodged in jail. Dipley is sullen and morose and had but little to say except that he murdered Ketchel in self-defense. But as Ketchel was shot from behind, no credence is taken to the story. A women by the name of Goldie Smith who went to the ranch with Dipley, claiming to be his wife, but who has since confessed that they were not married and that she was an eyewitness to the attack. Smith was arrested as an accomplice and is also confined in jail. The preliminary examination of Dipley and the Smith women will probably be held some time of the latter part of next week. Ketchel was taken to a hospital at Springfield Saturday afternoon where an operation was to have been performed in hopes of saving his life, but died soon after reaching there. John and Leon Ketchel picked up their brothers remains at the Paxton Funeral home and traveled back to Grand Rapids Michigan, near the home of their parents for burial.

Chapter 22:
The Funeral - A Touching Send Off

"Ketchel's funeral was perhaps the most touching exit of any fighter who ever lived." **-Nat Fleischer, founder of *Ring* magazine**

On the morning October 21, 1910, Grand Rapids, Michigan, held the biggest funeral in its history. Ketchel's family knew that he had lots of friends and thousands of fans, and were expecting a huge crowd. But their expectations were exceeded. Hype Igoe, Joe O'Connor and John, Leon and Alex Ketchel were pallbearers. The Following is an account of Ketchel's funeral from the October 21, 1910 edition of the *Grand Rapids Herald*:

> The last bell has sounded for Stanley Ketchel, middleweight champion pugilist of the world. Funeral services over the body of the murdered ring general were held yesterday morning at St. Adalbert's Church, (now called St. Adalbert's Basilica) which was packed to its greatest capacity; while the

streets about the church were crowded with men women and children, eager to catch a glimpse of the funeral procession and to gaze upon the gray hearse in which the one time idol of fistania was being taken on it's last journey. It is estimated that in the vicinity of 15,000 to 18,000 persons, from old women to infants in arms, a good many of whom were prompted with curiosity, gathered in the vicinity of the church long before the funeral cortege arrived and every available porch and step was pressed into service as a resting place. Never before in all of Grand Rapids history had such a crowd turned out to view the funeral procession of any man, no matter how great or famous he may have been. A drizzling rain set in early in the morning, but it did not serve to thin ranks of the crowd. The Polish Military band and carriages containing girls dressed in white, who carried flowers, waited for more than an hour at the corner of Leonard and Canal streets for the hearse and cortege which came overland from the family home near Pine Island Lake, near Belmont. The procession arrived about 10 o'clock, the grey hearse, drawn by white horses, followed by members of the local order of Elks and relatives in carriages. With the band play the funeral march, the line continued down Canal Street to Bridge, where it turned west and proceeded to Jefferson Street, thence to the church at Fourth and Davis Streets. Along the route of the procession the curbs were lined with hundreds of curious spectators, many of who followed along to the church, anxious to look upon the face of the slain fighter. When the cortege arrived at the church it was with great difficulty that the mourners and bearers of the casket made their way through the enormous crowd into the little edifice, which could not have held another person. The band played Chopin's funeral march while the body was being carried into the church....The solemn mass funeral service was said over the body by Father Skory and throughout the church complete silence reigned. The services lasted until 12:30 p.m., but the crowd outside did not diminish, for it was believed that a view of the dead man could be obtained. But the casket was not opened and the body was removed to the Polish Catholic Cemetery in Walker and interred.

It wasn't until late in the afternoon that the devastated crowd started to break up and move on with their lives. The middleweight championship was now vacant, and many Ketchel fans wondered who would be the next middleweight titleholder. Ketchel's championship belt was given to his family, who would hold it in their possession for years to come. For two years after his death, Ketchel had only a simple tombstone marking his grave, which read: Stanley Ketchel 1886-1910, SON. By 1912, friends and relatives were ready to put a larger monument over his grave. It is beautiful headstone, but it doesn't mention that Ketchel was a boxing champion. The following is a short article about Ketchel's new headstone from the Grand Rapids Sunday Morning Newspaper of Dec 1, 1912:

> As a tribute of loving and faithful friends a beautiful monument has been erected of the grave of Stanley Ketchel. Grand Rapids own, product of the fighting game at the New Polish Cemetery on North Street. Heretofore a pre-to the ravages of nature the final resting place, of the once great middleweight looms up from the roadside in majestic grandeur. Ketchel's name in full, the year of his birth and death all in fine cut oval letters are plainly visible to the passerby. By depriving themselves of many of necessities of life the dead champion's mother Julia and four son's John, Alexander, Leon and Arthur saved enough to have the monument built and placed over the grave. The die of the monument is finely hammered. The cap is of rock and tassels, and was built by Muste and Dykstra for the Ketchel relatives. Stanley Ketchel was shot and killed by Walter Dipley two years ago last October at the ranch just outside of Conway Missouri, and died soon as the result. There had

been much talk by many men of erecting a monument over his grave, but soon withered and it was left to the mother and sons to see that the grave of the son and brother should be properly taken care of. The base is 8' by 6' and the monument stands twelve and a half feet tall.

People have speculated as to what would have happened if Stanley Ketchel had lived. Maybe he would have continued defending his middleweight title or even accomplished his dream of becoming heavyweight champion. The world will never know. But one thing is certain: from 1903 to 1910, Ketchel had achieved something even greater than winning the middleweight title: he had become a legend. But it was the end of one event and the beginning of another. People across the country were waiting for the murder trial and conviction of Ketchel's killer, Walter S. Dipley, and his accomplice, Goldie Smith.

Chapter 23:
Walter and Goldie on Trial

The murder trial of Walter Dipley and Goldie Smith was the most talked about event in Missouri in 1911. Hundreds of people from Webster County and out of state would attend the trial in the old courthouse in Marshfield. The preliminary hearing for Dipley and Goldie was held on Thursday November 10, 1910, before Squire McCormack. Prosecuting attorney, A.H. Davis, of Webster County and his assistants, J.E. Haymes and Sam Dickey, represented the State. Also on the side of the State were R.P. Dickerson's special prosecutors, Roscoe and Orin Patterson, who were not related. A privately hired prosecuting attorney was legal in the early 20th century, and it wasn't until 1976, when the Missouri Supreme Court decided that it was "prejudiced and unfair", that the practiced ceased. Jefferson Delaney of Green County and George Clay of Joplin, Missouri, represented the defendants. Walter and Goldie were bound over for trial in the Circuit Court in the January term. Dipley was held without bail, while Goldie was given the chance to make $5,000 bond, but was unable to do so. Delaney was an earnest, talented lawyer, and he missed no opportunity to investigate laws and legal boundaries on behalf of his clients. Even before jury selection began, Delaney filed a proposal for action to disqualify Sheriff Shields.

"That man Shields should not be permitted to select or summon jurors or have any further conduct of the trial. The Sheriff is unduly biased and prejudiced in favor of the state and against the defendants," Delaney asserted.

By early December, twelve jurors had been selected. They were male farmers, married and mostly middle aged. Their names were J.A. Barnard, E.J. Moore, John Coughenour, Lyon George, J.O. Goodson, Elijah Clevenger, J.M. Miller, W.A. Wingo, Julien Jones, Elijah Carpenter, Oran Bell and F.M. Brown. Delaney complained about the way the jury was selected.

"Most of these men came from only two townships, the homes of the sheriff and the two prosecutors, which is not fair for our team and the defendants. The jury will automatically be prejudiced and I will not allow it," said Delaney.

Delaney found evidence that he felt would convince the court of Sheriff Shields' bias: an occurrence that took place three days before the trial was set to begin. On Friday, January 13th, R. P. Dickerson wrote a short letter to sheriff Shields:

> My Dear Sheriff Shields,
>
> They have the Ketchel – Johnson fighting pictures at the Grand Theater today and tomorrow. I would like to have you see them. Why not get a bunch of your friends and come up tomorrow and see them at my expense? They are good and I believe will help the good cause along. Try and come up tomorrow night and be my guest.
>
> Your Friend,
> R.P. Dickerson

According to the *Ozarks Melodrama*, in addition to the fight films, the evening at the Grand included "pictures thrown on the canvas" of the ranch house where Ketchel was shot, and of Dipley and Goldie, with a caption that read, "Killers of Stanley Ketchel." Shields and four of his friends from Marshfield watched the show at the Grand, but Shields said that he paid his own expenses: "We took a Kentucky treat and all paid for ourselves." Trial judge, C.H. Skinker, denied Delaney's motion to disqualify the sheriff. But Delaney later used the occurrence as one of many points in his plea for a new trial or change of venue.

After the inevitable petitions and counter petitions, the trial was set to begin. The State of Missouri vs. Walter S. Dipley and Goldie Smith commenced on Monday January 16, 1911. Both Dipley and Ketchel's family would attend the trial, with the Ketchel's traveling on a special train that was paid for by R.P. Dickerson. On the morning of the trial's first day, it was a struggle to enter the building due to the large number of reporters, newsmen and photographers; and the courtroom was packed to capacity. Dipley and Goldie sat together at the defense table with Jeff Delaney and George Clay. Across the room were the team of prosecuting attorneys, Roscoe and Orin Patterson, J.E. Haymes and Sam Dickey. Both sides were ready to do battle. The court was silent for several minutes as Judge C.H. Skinker came out of his chambers in a black robe and climbed the bench. The bailiff ordered the courtroom to rise, and as soon as Skinker seated himself, the bailiff ordered everyone to be seated.

"Good morning gentleman," Skinker said. "I hope both sides have prepared for their case. You've had two months to get ready and I hope it's done."

Both sides nodded their heads, signaling that they were ready.

"Alright then, lets proceed," continued Skinker. "The State of Missouri vs. Walter S. Dipley and Goldie Smith, who are charged for the murder of prizefighter, Stanley Ketchel, on October 15, 1910; now, before we go any further, which side would like to make the opening statement?"

The prosecution agreed to go first, and Roscoe Patterson rose to make the opening statement.

"May it please the court and you gentlemen of the jury, I will read you information in this case," said Patterson.

Delaney quickly rose to his feet and voiced objection. "The opening argument that Patterson just read must be made by the prosecuting attorney as prescribed by law. What he's doing is uncalled for."

Skinker upheld the objection. "Alright then, let's have Mr. Davis read the opening statement."

Delaney would go on to make hundreds of objections that were upheld by the judge. But of the over forty witnesses that would take the stand, none would be able to prove Dipley's plea of self-defense, which affirmed the prosecution's theory that Dipley approached Ketchel from behind and assassinated him. Without any eyewitness, the jury could only rely on Dipley and Goldie's version of what happened. And there would be much cross-examination about whether Ketchel had said, "they got me", or "he" got me. When C.E. Bailey and George Nolan took the stand, they both said that Ketchel replied, "They got me", thus confirming the prosecution's theory that Goldie was involved.

The court would hear Dipley and Goldie tell their side of the story of what happened before and during the morning of October 15, 1910. Dipley was the first to take the stand. He testified that, on October 13, he borrowed Ketchel's rifle to kill animals. He testified that he and Goldie spent Thursday night at Dickerson's ranch in a little log house and were getting ready to move to the main house to help Ketchel the next day. One the morning following their first night on the ranch, Dipley said that he used Ketchel's rifle to kill a chicken.

"We weren't eating so good on the ranch, we had nothing but canned goods," he testified.

Delaney asked Dipley what happened after he shot the chicken.

"This man named Brazeale, a cropper who lived on the ranch, asked me what I was shooting at and I told him a groundhog. I said 'Can't you see it down the hill there?' He said no, he couldn't see it. I said, 'I suppose it went into a hole.' I says, 'Do you suppose that gun would kill a man?' He said he would rather be shot by a .44. I went into the basement of the barn, and told him I was going to feed and I come out and got the chicken and took it to the house," Dipley said.

"You didn't want him to know you had killed the chicken?" asked Delaney.

"No sir. It was one of R.P. Dickerson's chickens. I worked in the fields all day that Friday planting wheat. Goldie cooked the chicken and cleaned the main house. Later that day Goldie moved our things from the log house to the main house, and Ketchel, I think, helped her. When I returned from the fields about 6 o'clock that evening, I noticed Goldie was acting strangely."

"And what did she say to you?" asked Delaney.

"I asked her what was wrong; she said nothing was the matter. I asked her two or three times, and then she said Ketchel had made some bad threats. She said, 'I want to leave here.' After dinner Goldie and I went over to talk to foreman Bailey. He was leaving the ranch the next morning. I asked Bailey if Goldie and I could ride to Conway with him the next day. He said yes. He said, 'What is the trouble?' I says, 'I have quit.' I told him that there hadn't been any trouble, but I was leaving to prevent trouble."

"So, after planning to travel to Conway with Bailey the next day, you returned to the house. Did Goldie that night tell you what had taken place?" asked Delaney.

"Yes sir, she told me Ketchel threw her on across the bed and tried to take her clothes off and have sexual intercourse with her."

"And then what happened?" asked Delaney.

The prosecution immediately objected to the testimony, complaining that it was completely immaterial. The objection was sustained under the reasoning that Goldie should tell of the events herself. Delaney spoke softly to Goldie, trying to make her seem as innocent as possible, and Goldie rose to the occasion, conjuring up tears as she told of how Ketchel had supposedly ravished her.

"What did he do to you?" asked Delaney.

"He threw me on the bed and accomplished the biggest part of what he undertook."

"He threw you on the bed? Why is that? For what purpose?" Delaney asked.

"I don't know what you call it."

"Use the words," Delaney prodded. "What did he throw you on the bed for, to have sexual intercourse with you?"

"Yes sir, Mr. Ketchel said that he would kill me and Walter if we told anybody he threatened me with his gun."

Roscoe Patterson didn't believe that Ketchel accosted Goldie. "Why didn't you call for help, why didn't you halloo?" he questioned her.

"I was afraid to halloo because I was frightened he would kill me, he had his gun on him."

"And you thought he would kill you?" Patterson asked.

"Yes sir, then he threw me on the bed and that's where he done the rest."

"Were your clothes torn any?" asked Patterson.

"No, sir."

"Not even a scratch or bruise?" Patterson continued.

"No, Sir."

"Well, did he have intercourse with you and you were just laying there on the bed?" asked Patterson.

"No, I didn't."

"Did you struggle any?" Paterson prodded.

"Yes, Sir. I fought him all I could."

"Was there any marks on him when you got through?" asked Patterson.

"Well Sir, I don't know. I didn't look to see."

"Is it not a fact, Miss Smith, that you became enamored of him and that you yourself made sexual overtures to him, and Ketchel rejected you? So you became upset and you waited for Mr. Dipley to return home from the fields to make some false fabrication that Ketchel insulted you and raped you because you knew that Dipley had a short fuse. Is that a fact, Miss Smith?" pressured Patterson.

Goldie was at a loss for words and hesitated for a moment. Then she replied, "no sir, that is not a fact."

Goldie testified that, on Saturday morning, October 15th, she and Walter got up at 4:30 a.m., and that she fixed their breakfast, and that Dipley went out to feed Dickerson's horses even though he'd be leaving with Bailey that morning.

"I knew the boys would be after the horses to take out to work," Walter would later explain when he was back on the stand.

Goldie said that Dipley came back to the house and ate breakfast with her after feeding the horses. "It was about six o' clock," Goldie remembered. "It wasn't hardly daylight yet."

She testified that Ketchel came out of his bedroom to the front porch, and that he had a .45 Colt revolver in his waistband, and that the rifle that Dipley had borrowed from him was at the end of the bed in the spare room that she shared with Dipley. She said that, after eating his breakfast, Dipley went to the front porch to smoke a cigarette, and that

Ketchel went into the dining room and sat down at the north end of the table, with his back facing the kitchen door, at which time she served him breakfast. Dipley finished his cigarette and entered the house, she said, and that was as much as she knew for sure. Now it was time for Dipley to explain what occurred that morning.

When asked if Ketchel had spoken to him prior to the shooting, Dipley replied that Ketchel had questioned him, "what the hell are you doing around that this time of day? Why ain't you out in the fields working?" To which Dipley replied, "Why, I am not going out in the fields today, I have quit."

Dipley then said that Ketchel questioned Dipley's poor attitude: "What in the hell is the matter with you this morning?" To which Dipley responded, "I suppose you are awful damned innocent that you don't know what is the matter."

"Don't you start anything or I will give you some of this," Ketchel supposedly replied, opening his shirt and showing Dipley his gun.

"I guess you would give me some of that alright," Dipley purportedly responded, to which Ketchel said, "Yes, goddamn you, if you start anything I will shoot you in two."

"Will you?" Dipley said he questioned him, and then grabbed the rifle that was sitting nearby.

"Where did he have his hand when you grabbed the rifle?" Delaney asked Dipley.

"In his bosom; he put his hand in his bosom when he said, 'If you start anything, I will shoot you in two.' I grabbed the little rifle at the corner there and jumped back into the kitchen backwards or sideways, I don't recall. Ketchel was standing at the time. He got up from the table and was standing and looking over his left shoulder and had his gun in his bosom. I told him, I says, 'Throw up your hands,' or 'take your hand off your gun,' I don't remember which it was. I said, 'You are under arrest.' Ketchel said, 'By god, I won't.' Then I shot him."

After Dipley's account of the shooting, Goldie again took the stand under cross-examination by Roscoe Patterson, giving an account of what was said after the shooting. "My Husband told Ketchel to take his hand off his gun; he said, 'No by god, I won't.' Then he shot, that was all."

"So, Mr. Dipley just went right over to Mr. Ketchel and shot him?" asked Patterson.

"I think so. Yes, to the best of my knowledge."

"Did you make any exclamation, Miss Smith?" Asked Patterson.

"I says, 'Please Mr. Ketchel, don't shoot Walter. That is what I said. After Mr. Ketchel was shot, he stumbled past me into the middle room and fell. I ran to the front porch, my husband went out the back door."

"You ran out the front porch and then what happened?" Patterson asked.

"I ran to the front porch. Then I heard a noise back in the house and I come back in. I thought my husband was in there with him. I run back in and went to the door of the kitchen there and just as I got there, I seen my husband right there, and I knew he wasn't in the other room. My husband said to me, 'Come on mamma, Let's go.'"

"He said 'come on let's go'?" asked Patterson.

"Yes sir. Then he went back in there and picked up the gun and taken it with him."

Dipley would later testify that he took Ketchel's gun because he was frightened that Ketchel would revive and use the weapon on he and Goldie. It was "self-defense" Dipley kept repeating. But Judge Skinker himself was skeptical about Walter and Goldie's account. Neither was the jury buying their story. The trial lasted eight days, and on Tuesday, January 24, 1911, the defense and prosecution were ready to start their closing arguments. The last day of trial was an important day in Webster

County. Schools were closed and people didn't go to work so they stand outside the courthouse. The courtroom and its narrow aisles were jammed for the closing arguments. Dipley's parents and three brothers were in their seats, and the Ketchel family was seated right across from them.

According to the *Marshfield Chronicle*, "a flow of oratory such as has never been heard in the old courthouse before" became the closing arguments.

A.H. Davis delivered the state's closing argument, stressing Dipley's desertion from the Navy and Goldie's scandalous lifestyle describing her as a "vile creature" and "devoid of all principle of pure womanhood."

Davis argued that Goldie and Dipley's account of killing in self-defense was a complete fabrication. "Miss. Smith had deliberately placed Ketchel at the breakfast table with his back to the kitchen door. Dipley then came in the kitchen door and stealthily approached Ketchel from behind and assassinated him, stealing his ring, his money and his gun. No argument took place, it was not self-defense but murder, willful and premeditated. Death is the appropriate penalty!"

When Delaney addressed the jury, he claimed that, "Dipley had a right to shoot Ketchel, for it was self-defense. Ketchel was going to murder Goldie and Walter with his revolver. Mr. Dipley believed that Ketchel was about to draw his weapon. He was afraid for his life and shot in self-defense. Miss Smith should not be considered part of the shooting at all, and should be acquitted and never serve time in jail."

After closing arguments, Judge Skinker delivered his final instructions to the jury: "Whether or not Goldie Smith was actually assaulted by Stanley Ketchel has little or no bearing on the outcome. Even if you believe that Ketchel did assault or ravish Miss Smith, you cannot use heat of passion to reduce the charge against Dipley from first degree murder to second-degree murder, and, furthermore, you must find Walter Dipley guilty of first-degree murder. If you gentlemen come to a conclusion that Goldie Smith in any way had encouraged the murder or had any knowledge of it, you jurymen should return a verdict of first-degree murder for both defendants."

Walter and Goldie's fates were in the hands of the jury, and they were taken back to their cells. C.E. Bailey, while waiting for the verdict with R.P. Dickerson and the Ketchel's in the crowded hall outside the courtroom, remarked about Dipley and Goldie's testimony, "I didn't believe a word they said. Anybody who steals money, jewelry and pistol whips a man who is badly wounded is not self-defense."

The jury deliberated for 17 hours. Then they told Judge Skinker they had reached a unanimous verdict. Once word got out that a verdict had been reached, the people hurried back to the courtroom. The defense and prosecution came out of the judge's chambers and took their seats, and the judge seated himself on the bench. Walter and Goldie were brought in and placed at the defense table by Delaney and Clay. The room was suddenly quiet as it waited for judge Skinker to speak.

"Jurors, look upon the defendants; defendants look upon the jurors. How say you 12 gentlemen of the jury: do you find the prisoners, Walter S. Dipley and Goldie Smith, guilty or not guilty of the murder of Stanley Ketchel?"

"Guilty of murder in the first degree!" hollered the jury foreman.

Dipley appeared surprised at the verdict, but Goldie showed no emotion. Sobs were heard throughout the courtroom. The verdict would soon be known everywhere across the U.S. The following is an article from the January 26th, 1911 edition of the *Marshfield Chronicle*:

> Motion for a new trial will be made, but it is thought will be refused by, the court, in which event an appeal will be made to the Supreme Court. The verdict of the jury returned Tuesday before noon at 11:30 o'clock declared Walter S.

Dipley and Goldie Smith guilty of murder in the first degree and sentenced them to life imprisonment for the murder of Stanley Ketchel, champion middleweight pugilist of the world. The announcement of the jury that a verdict had been reached was a surprise to many as it was not though that an agreement could be reached in so short a time. The finding of the jury was also a complete surprise to a large majority, as it was not thought that Dipley would receive a punishment more than murder in the second-degree and many thought he would be freed. The surprise was greatest regarding Goldie Smith as scarcely anyone thought she would be convicted but freed of charge. The arguments were finished Monday evening and the instructions given to the jury. They spent about two hours discussing the instructions and at an early hour Tuesday morning commenced their deliberations and continued until about 11 o'clock when the first and only vote was taken. A large crowd was in the courtroom at the time the verdict was announced as had been at all times since the trial commenced. No excitement or demonstration was exhibited and the defendants, who had been brought to the courtroom to hear the verdict read, dropped their heads. When Dipley's two brothers, Albert and Amos spoke to him about the decision of the jury, he said, "I am very surprised," but the woman who had posed as his wife seemed to look at it in a different view and said, "It is nothing more than I expected." They were taken to prison by Sheriff Shields to await the further action of the court. Dipley's father and mother, who had been here ever since the trial commenced, were not in the courtroom at the time the verdict was read. Motion for a new trial based on alleged errors of the court during the trial, will be filed tomorrow or Saturday by attorneys of the defense. The motion was quite a lengthy document, it is said, and if refused an appeal will be taken to the Supreme Court. The attorneys feel confident in the out come of their motion for a new trial and it is said cites some of the following errors: That Judge Skinker refused to give instructions asked by the attorneys for the defendants; that if the story of the alleged assault on Ketchel on Goldie Smith was communicated by Dipley, it was a fact that should have been considered by the court in the instructions of the jury; the attorneys contend that if such fact is either true or untrue, if it was communicated to Dipley, was a fact to be considered as throwing light on the question as to whether or not a controversy arose between Ketchel and the defendant, Dipley in order to explain their attitude at the time of the difficulty; that if Ketchel made bad threats against Dipley and such threats were communicated to Dipley, he had a right in the controversy with Ketchel to act upon less appearances of danger than if such threats had not been communicated; that the fact that Goldie Smith and Dipley were living together as immoral life and that he had deserted the U.S. Navy did not impair in any way his right to self defense: that the court erred in permitting Sheriff Shields and his deputies to summon the talisman, because the Sheriff accepted an invitation from R.P. Dickerson to attend the moving picture show of the Ketchel –Johnson fight in Springfield; also that 80 percent of the jurors of the special panel were selected from the homes of prosecuting attorney A.H. Davis and attorney J.E. Haymes, and attorneys for the state: that the testimony of George Nolan and C.E Bailey, that Ketchel's dying statement was "I Guess they got me," when in the preliminary hearing they said it was "I guess he got me," is objected too, and the last statement will be pushed because it is thought it will help the woman should a reversal of the decision be reached. The attorneys for the state, of course, are well pleased with the verdict, while the attorneys for the defense are surprised that a much lighter sentence was not given to Dipley, and the woman acquitted. The Defendants are convicted and the jurors all farmers, seven Baptists – four Methodists and one no church. Both sides made a hard fight and the case was bitterly contested from beginning to end. The attorneys for the state left no stone unturned it would seem a conviction of the man and women, while the attorneys for the defense were equally aggressive in their work to exonerate the accused pair. The first witness in this case was examined Thursday afternoon of last week. There were about 80 witnesses subpoenaed but only 40 of them were used. The trial continued from that time till Saturday evening including night sessions examining the witnesses. Court then adjourned until Monday morning, which the lawyers spent presenting their arguments to the jury with great oratory. The evidence upon which Dipley and Goldie Smith, were convicted is to the effect that Dipley shot the middleweight champion from behind at the breakfast table in the morning of October 15, 1910. Webster County people took a highly creditable stand for the reign of law in the verdict, which twelve citizens returned in the Dipley case. That County has done few things more calculated to show the love of the people for morality than in decreeing that two persons who set the laws of right living ruthlessly aside shall be placed where they cannot contaminate others, even though they become no better themselves. The whole bearing of the residents of Webster County during the sensational happenings, which began with the Ketchel murder and found culmination in the conviction and sentencing of the slayers was commendable in the best sense. The public mind, there was singularly free from bias, and the utterances of the people relative to the crime and the circumstance surrounding it's commission revealed only the sincere wish that entire justice might be done. It was this feeling, which made the trial possible in that county, which assured the accused pair absolute safety while their fate at the hands of the court was unknown, and which now guarantees the carrying out the decrees of the law free of any interference from other influences. Unprejudiced people everywhere must feel that the cause of justice has had full sway in Webster County in this matter. There is not a section of the state that cannot with profit study the lesson which the attitude of the people there presents in this tragedy. As the Ketchel – Dipley case has consumed six out of the nine days of the circuit court since it commenced until we go to press this week, the Mail has decided to wait until court closes and then give the disposition of the docket in detail. This will probably be in our next issue.

Jeff Delaney repeatedly filed motions for a new trial, but the motions were denied. Then the case was appealed to the Missouri Supreme Court, which ended in Goldie's favor. In May 1912, after serving 17 months in the penitentiary, Goldie Smith walked out of jail a free woman. The Supreme Court declared that the State failed to prove beyond a reasonable doubt that there was a conspiracy to murder Stanley Ketchel, and that she had had no part in the attack. Dipley, on the other hand, continued to serve his life sentence. During his first years in prison, he had a record of bad behavior, including fights with other prisoners and possession of narcotics. Later, Dipley started mending and making shoes for other convicts, and did so until his release. R.P. Dickerson and the Ketchel's fought attempts to obtain parole for Dipley. They maintained that such a brutal crime suggested that the killer could not be fit for release. However, on Saturday May 19, 1934, Missouri Governor, Guy B. Parks, granted Dipley parole.

"The man had a fantastic record for good behavior in prison," said Parks, referring to the latter part of Dipley's sentence. After serving 23 years, Dipley was free man. But he continued to live a troubled life. There are two records of marriages for Dipley in Jasper County, MO: Isabel Saunders on February 25, 1940, which ended in divorce not long after, and Ola M. Cupp on September 13, 1947, which lasted only 30 days. Cupp filed for divorce because Walter was alcoholic, abusive, gambled, used horrible language and went to places unknown after only 30 days of marriage. Dipley had no children and there is no record that he and Goldie ever married. According to one story, after receiving news of Dipley's release, the 45-year-old Goldie blushed, giggled and broke into a kind of dance. A newsman from Springfield asked her how she felt about the news. "Man," she hollered, "you don't know how glad I am!"

When asked if she could locate Dipley, she replied that, if she knew where he was, she would be on a bus headed there. The reporter then asked her if she and Dipley had ever been married.

"No," she replied. "He came to my home with me after I met him in Webb City, Missouri. He said, if I'd do him a favor, that he'd marry me. So I did."

In 1956, Walter Dipley passed away from kidney disease and was buried in an unmarked grave in a Toquerville, Utah Cemetery. In Springfield, Goldie became a manager of a small Café located at Boonville Hill. She married a fourth time to "Gentleman" Jim Hooper, a well-known gambler in the area. Hooper later became a barber, but made a poor living for the couple. After Hooper's death in March 1934, Goldie made a living selling trinkets from her front porch at 627 Boonville Street. The date of her death is unknown.

In 1914, the men who captured Dipley didn't receive the $5,000 reward because Dickerson wanted him dead and not alive. The Hoggard brothers and Zib Murphy took Dickerson to court, and after long, bitter litigation, the court ordered Dickerson to not only pay the reward with interest, which totaled of $5,612.50. Dickerson continued to lead a colorful life. When the United States was involved in World War I, it brought out Dickerson's patriotism, and he volunteered to help create a regiment called the "Rough Riders", which would be composed of the United States' best sportsmen. The offer fell through, but Dickerson did run a large mule ranch and supplied the U.S. army with the healthiest mules. Dickerson died in 1938.

Chapter 24:
The Prophecy: "I won't live to be 30!"

In 1909, Stanley Ketchel made a prophecy that he would not live to be 30 years old. Whether or not he was serious in his prediction is a mystery. But, according to some of his friends, Ketchel became grim when he talked of the possibility of dying at an early age, and always said that he would die in a car accident because of his love for speed. Hype Igoe would be the first to talk about Ketchel's strange prediction to Nat Fleischer. Fleischer put Igoe's account in his own biography of Ketchel, "The Michigan Assassin: The saga of Stanley Ketchel", published in 1946. Igoe would later become a successful New York boxing writer and journalist. The following is his account to Fleischer of his experiences with Ketchel and Ketchel's morbid prophecy:

> One of the greatest fistic characters I had ever met was Stanley Ketchel. We were pals inseparable. I trained with him, traveled with him and loved him as I would my own child. My associations with this great fighter, the greatest middleweight boxing has ever seen, enabled me to study

him more closely than even his own folks. He was a many - sided individual. He could be as tame as a new born babe, as vicious as a lion trying to protect its cubs, as lovable as a mother and as treacherous as an uncouth villain about to strike the unguarded prey. I never knew him to sit down to a meal in any big town without first laying his blue six-shooter across his lap. I never could quite understand just why he went so armed. I nearly died of anxiety in Wheeling, West, Virginia, one morning, when we went down to breakfast in the Clark House. Now mind you nobody had made any threats against Ketchel so far as I knew. He had fought Frank Klaus in Pittsburgh a few nights before and so badly injured the thumb on his left hand that the fist was swollen to five time it's normal size. Ketchel was to open in a sparring and bag punching turn in conjunction with Sam Howe's 'burlesque' company and our problem was how to fashion a pillow around that horribly puffed hand so that the cash customers wouldn't be any wiser. Ketchel had hit Klaus high on the head with the first left hook and as the blow landed, Klaus said tauntingly: 'you bashed your hand that time, didn't you Stanley'? Ketchel didn't have to be reminded about what happened. He wasn't in any too good condition as it was, having just come from Hot Springs after a six - month layoff following his knockout defeat by Jack Johnson. 'Yes I busted my hand,' snarled Ketchel, "but I'll lick you with the other one... and he did. We came down to breakfast and Ketchel was in an ugly mood. His swollen hand was giving him fits and chances are that he was fixing to get even with the world. One of the black waiters gave Ketchel a very snippy answer about the kind of eggs, pancakes, and bacon they had on tap and I saw Stanley reach for the gun under the tablecloth. 'Here it comes,' I mused. 'We'll both die in the electric chair for what is about to come. I've got to bluff my way out of this one.' I bit into my thin water glass and cut my mouth, purposely, and with blood running from my lips I yelled for Ketchel to see me to the washroom. He stuck his blue gun into his pants waistband and hustled me off to the washroom. I insisted that I was bleeding to death and he must hustle me out of the hotel and to a doctor. Anything to get away from that waiter, and the ruse worked, tender as a woman now, his whole concern was about my cut lip. I had slyly bitten into it to make it worse, anything to get Ketchel from flying into a rage about the waiter. We finished our coffee and rolls elsewhere and for the three day's, during which we remained in dear Old Wheeling, I studiously objected to the food at the Clark house, though in truth they were noted for their splendid table, for supper we ate Chinese food. That blue gun still bulged under Ketchel's superbly tailored coat of his $150 Fifth Avenue suit. Later on Ketchel had a soft heart and later apologized to the waiter. The odd part about Ketchel's death is that he predicted that he would die before he was thirty. Because of his habit of driving his expensive motorcars at terrific speed, he himself really thought that he was destined to fade out in a motor-car crash. He hadn't come around to aviation as yet or an unhappy landing might have been his farewell to earth. He was daring, picturesque and death held no fears for him. I sat beside him late one night as he was driving a big Lozier car at 78 miles an hour in a blinding rainstorm back to his training camp at Woodlawn Inn, N.Y. He was in a winding treacherous car track, with steel electric light poles studding the ground between the two tracks every few yards. Those poles were singing behind us like strings on a great harp. I fancied that they were playing our 'Requiem' cold beads of perspiration ran down my face like buckshot. This was the end. 'Old timer, I'll die before I'm thirty!' How those words roared in my ears now! This speed madman was deliberately racing us toward eternity, taking the old timer with him! I leaned toward his ear and above the din of the racing motor I shouted: 'Hey Stan, suppose we skid?' Ketchel bellowed, 'It will be too late for supposing!' I resumed my death - watch, any moment now surely he'd lose control on one of those greasy curves. I could see one of the poles cutting us in twain as we skidded and I closed my eyes and prepared for death, there was so precious little time left. I must have passed out because the next thing I knew Ketchel the speed demon was shaking me with: 'Come on, wake up old timer, home, sweet home.' The juggernaut had come to a standstill and I could feel the heat from the motor, as it seemed to be panting for breath. There was a cemetery next to where we quartered and as I crawled out of my seat I wondered over what sort of miracle had spared my best friends and relatives from have to purchase one of those large monuments for us. Ketchel used to drive a carmine colored automobile in San Francisco and one day he came down a steep hill just as a Chinese laundry wagon crossed his path. There was no stopping or whipping out of danger. Ketchel, on the fraction of the instant decided that he must hit the horse and wagon head-on to prevent his car turning turtle. He hit the rig alright! Those who saw it say that both horse and the heathen Chinese started for heaven at the same time only in different directions. There weren't even enough splinters left to make a box of matches. Ketchel left San Francisco rather hurriedly that day. He kept right on toward the ferry and was back in New York before the Chinaman old horse came back to earth. Ketchel always had a very tender side. He was terrific in his likes and dislikes. Perhaps the person he really liked more than anyone else was a quiet character who haunted his training camps, Pete 'the Goat' Stone, who acted as a chore boy for the middleweight champion. One day at Woodlawn Inn training camp Ketchel wanted to take a little snooze. A message came for Ketchel and Pete went up to his room and knocked on the door. 'Get away from that door,' growled Ketchel. 'A message for you open up,' came back Pete, and then came a loud deafening report. A bullet from the famous six-shooter crashed through the door and into the Goat's leg. He yelled in agony and fell while clutching the yellow telegram. The door flew open and a horrified Stanley Ketchel looked down at the one person he really liked. He immediately picked up Pete in his powerful arms and raced down the stairs and into his automobile. Still holding Pete in his lap, Ketchel raced at breakneck speed to the hospital and crying profusely along the way. He kept begging and pleading the 'Goat' to forgive him, which Pete did. Peter idolized Stanley and later said: 'It was well worth the bullet in the leg to be cuddled like a baby in the arms of the greatest fist fighter who ever lived!' Ketchel stayed in the operating room all night while the doctors were examining Pete. When the "Goat was well enough to go home Ketchel carried him out just like he carried him in, tenderly as a mother holds her child. Both have gone on the great adventure, Pete following the dashing champion years afterward. Peter became interested in night - clubs and was rated one of the wealthiest men on Broadway. He had a huge bankroll and a collection of jewels, deposits made on loans to New York's Broadway gamblers and men about town. The chances are Pete hid his fortune away in some vault and the money was unclaimed for many years. The night after the bout with Klaus in Pittsburgh we were in one of the leading cafes, with a great crowd of barflies in Ketchel's wake. Ketchel ordered a quart of imported champagne for everyman in the house and some who had slid up to a place at the long bar had never quaffed bubble water. Ketchel decided to have a little rough fun at their expense. He and I were standing at the end of the bar and the bartenders were working feverishly to pop some fifty bottles of the grape, the bottles standing like soldiers along the bar. I had never seen so much champagne in my life. When all the bottles had been uncorked, paid for and the first drink of the sizzling stuff poured, Ketchel, to the utter amazement of the big crowd, went along the bar knocking over the sputtering bottles right and left with giant swings of his arms. They crashed on the marble floor of the café. Ketchel backed to the door with myself making a hasty getaway ahead of him. 'You bums want to ruin your stomachs with that stuff? Go back to beer where you belong,' shouted Ketchel, as he, too, made his quick exit. Stanley Ketchel was quite a character.

Fleischer, who interviewed Ketchel several times and became his close acquaintance, also had stories to tell about him:

> Ketchel was a superstitious type and believed in signs. If someone threw a hat on his bed or opened an umbrella in the house, Stanley would throw forty fits. He invariably made it a point to shake hands with all of his seconds before the bell rang and Pete "the Goat" Stone, his chore boy and chief second, was the last one whose hand he'd grasp. Ketchel wasted no time with press agents nor did he make any grudges against color, weight, or reputation of his opponents. He was ever ready to meet all comers. He was a man of whims, yet he made friends readily He was bashful to an extraordinary degree. At times his bashfulness amounted almost to timidity. In conversation with newly arrived scribes or visitors to his camp, he would speak in monosyllables but once he became thoroughly acquainted, he was one of the gang. His frank open eyes were soft, but the moment he climbed through the ropes in pursuit of his prey, those eyes became the eyes of a ferocious animal bent on destroying his man. He fought with his mouth close tightly, a slight grin of disdain on his face and he breathed always through his nostrils. He scorned the word retreat, once his mission was over and he either flattened his opponent or won the verdict, he was just one of the mob a man full of fun and mischief, the transformation was electric. It has been said of Ketchel that he didn't have any nerves. I wish the people who started those stories could have been in the Ketchel training camp on the day or night before any of his fights. The ordinarily good-natured and frolicsome Ketchel became as sour and crabbed as a wounded grizzly bear. The fellows didn't dare say, 'boo' to him, and took great pains to keep out of his way. He would have a fit of temper at the least provocation. Ketchel was all stone and ice and concentration when he entered the ring. In a few hours leading up to ring time, however he was as cross as a sick old women. When Ketchel fought Porky Flynn in

Boston and knocked Porky colder than the proverbial mackerel in the third round, Flynn's brother commenced to throw water on him, in violation of the rules. Pete Stone, Ketchel's chief of staff, yelled for referee Flahtery to stop the violation. "Shut up Pete," demanded Ketchel, then to the surprise of all, he grabbed his own pail of water, raced across the ring and dumped the entire contents of that bucket on Porky's head. 'See,' exclaimed Stanley to Porky's brother, as Flynn never stirred under the deluge, 'When I put them out, they stay out!' Ketchel had a lazy, easygoing way of pulling away from a punch, and the fact his handsome features were unmarred to the end of his days was proof that his opponents didn't hit him as often as it appeared they did. I met Philadelphia Jack O'Brien two days after his famous fight with Ketchel in New York in Considine's Old Meeting House at 42nd Street and Broadway. O'Brien was drinking broth. I mentioned the fact. 'There's a reason, Nat,' said O'Brien. 'You people are always saying that Ketchel is crude and not clever. Let me tell you something: I've met all the clever men of my time and yours. I know skill and cleverness when I meet it. I'm supposed to be a bit nifty on that score myself. I want to inform you that in all my career, I've never met a fellow a clever as Ketchel! He surely doesn't look so, he seems crude and easy to hit and isn't at all to my surprise. He left jabbed me on the mouth more times that I've ever been poked in all my career. I just couldn't get away from his left. I kept trying to beat him to it, and you fellows were crediting me with scoring when it was Ketchel's left that always was banging against my teeth. Look here, if you don't think he landed his left, look at this!' O'Brien took both hands and opening his mouth he lifted his upper lip away from his teeth and turned it up. It was the most cruelly lacerated lip I've ever seen. I've never seen such a horrible memento of a fight. 'I guess he didn't jab me none,' commented O'Brien dryly. Now you know why I'm drinking broth instead of eating a big steak. This is the first nourishment I've had in two days. He jabbed and punched my appetite back to my nursing bottle days. I've never met a cleverer man than Stanley Ketchel,' concluded O'Brien. And we boxing fans thought Stanley was foolishly aggressive, easy to hit, utterly devoid of cleverness! Among the pranks practiced in training camp by Ketchel, was the famous snipe hunt, which for originality, the laughter it brought to those on the "in" and the distress and discomfiture it brought to the victim, took the cake. Stanley had a weird sense of humor. When in New York, he would do his training at Woodlawn, not far from the entrance of the Woodlawn Cemetery. The adjoining territory was wild, with tall grass, huge trees and a few houses within a radius of several miles. It was one of the undeveloped portions of the city, an ideal location for training. It was there that Ketchel took delight in luring sparring mates and other hangers-on for his well know snipe hunt, usually Ketchel would first make certain that he had the confidence of those he intended to lure into the woods, by joking, storytelling and engaging them in card games. Then, when he spotted his man, invariably the most talkative of the lot, he would nod a wink to the boys, and politely ask his companion to accompany him to the training table where the arrangements for the hunt were made. 'How would you like to join me in a snipe hunt, tomorrow' Stanley would ask. What a silly query! The honor of supping with the famous Michigan Assassin was glory in itself, but to stalk the woods in Ketchel's company at night for the elusive snipe was an experience the sucker would always cherish! At least so he thought! The next day, dinner over, the great hunt was on. A lone miner's lantern was the only means of finding the trail through the woods. The victim's was provided with a potato sack. Into this sack Ketchel and the scouts proposed to drive the wary snipe. A snipe potpie was to be the culmination of the hunt and the victim was told that he must not permit the snipe to pass him on the trail once Ketchel and his buddies started off the birds. A snipe, he was told, would never change his course after starting the trail. The snipe trail was found after a long shin-scratching jaunt through the briars. 'Now you remain here, and keep the mouth of the bag open right in the middle of the path,' said Ketchel. 'The snipe will see the chirping that is now going on in the brush, there should be several dozen of them on the loose tonight. Mind now, remain on guard, keep that bag wide open and keep your eyes open, remember be on guard!' Ketchel would then pick up his lantern and go off with the others, leaving his companion snipe snarer holding the bag, and holding it he certainly was! Ketchel and his companions would go back to the Inn by a roundabout way and start a card came, lasting until midnight. Then Ketchel in a sympathetic tone would laugh it off and retire for the night, letting the poor chap in the wilds find his way out of his predicament. Never would Stanley or his pals relieve the victim. The sniper would come to the Inn during the early morning hours and find it closed for the night. Those gloomy darkened windows seemed to laugh at him to tell him that he had been kidded. Usually Ketchel and his companions would never again hear about the hunter and that was one sure way of eliminating the pest from the camp. Occasionally, however, there would be some persistent cuss who would come back the next day and seek out the great middleweight. In the latter case, the victim would lament his ill fortune only to get a bawling out from Stanley for apparently 'disobeying' his orders and Ketchel would tell him that, because of his negligence in not doing as he was told, the hunters lost all the snipe. And that evening immediately following dinner, out on the trail again would go the fighter and his buddies to give the pest another little 'trick.' Stanley Ketchel, was quite playful indeed!

Fleischer brought *Ring Magazine* to fame in 1922, and he published the "Bible of Boxing" until his death in 1972. In April 1969, controversy was raging over who would win between Ketchel and Sugar Ray Robinson. According to a computer simulation, Robinson won a close decision, with his boxing skill and hand speed enabling him to pile up points and barely survive Ketchel's raging attacks. However, many experts who saw both Ketchel and Robinson in their prime were of the opinion that Ketchel's endurance (he could still deliver knockout blows after 32 rounds) would have prevailed. Fleischer had a good reason why Ketchel would have defeated Robinson:

> I want to say that while I no longer am 39 years of age, I am not one of the old men always fighting for the days of long ago and what they meant. Not that the days of yore were entirely to be despised even if they had no television and no heavyweight champion for refusing to answer the draft. I want to make it clear to all that I was one of the first boxing writers to recognize Ray Robinson as a great technician, one of the first to acclaim him as true champion after his welterweight championship victory over Tommy Bell in 1946. But Ray Robinson could not have beaten Stanley Ketchel. Stan knocked out fighters who would have beaten Robinson with both contestants in their prime form. Ketchel would have had a big edge over Robinson in explosive power and infighting. I say this in no disparagement of Ray. The art of inflicting punishment and scoring points in close almost had died out of boxing, and that is doubly bad. Robinson would have an edge in footwork. Ray would have an edge in hurting his man while punching going away. But you analyze Robbie's record and he was too prideful ever to enter a ring without giving all he had. Robinson would have had, as major assets against Ketchel, fast hands. Faster hands than Stan, but the old power agent would have been predominantly on the side of the Assassin. Seeing a Robinson-Ketchel fight in my minds eye, I find the Assassin swarming all over the sugar man with diabolical fury, which was a major characteristic and trademark of the scion of the polish Kiecals. Robinson beat Ketchel? Maybe, and then again, maybe not. In fact, No!

In an August 8, 1982, an article by Tom Lebelle for the Grand Rapids press mentioned New York sports writer, John D. McCallum's, interesting story about Mickey Walker; king of the middleweights in the late 1920's. Walker entered a New York bar after winning a big fight and was approached by an adoring drunk. "Kid, you're the greatest middleweight who ever came down the road," the drunk said. "The greatest. And don't let anybody tell you different." Then someone in the bar hollered, "What about Ketchel?" Instantly, the drunk ceased to adore. He seized Walker's coat and said, "Listen, you bum, you couldn't lick one side of Stanley Ketchel on the best day you ever saw." To Walker's amazement, the entire bar agreed. Robert Edgren, a well-known boxing writer during Ketchel's hey day, had nothing but praise for the ex-champion: "Ketchel was natural born fighter. He was a mixer; always ready to swap punches, confident that the ones he gave would do more damage than the ones he received. He could take a punch to land one. He had the strength and pugnacity of a wild beast and would rather fight than eat."

In September 1961, the youngest Ketchel brother, Arthur, would send letters to boxing writers that had published inaccuracies about Ketchel's life. Arthur, who was only eight years old when his brother was murdered, had memories that showed Ketchel was not simply the "killer" that people said he was. Stanley Weston, a well-known boxing writer, put Arthur's story in a 1961 issue of *Boxing Illustrated*, of which the following is an excerpt:

> Stanley Ketchel looked down at me as we stood in the doorway of Detroit's biggest department store. He gestured at the counters piled high with goods and toys and all sorts of wonderful things. "Pick out anything in the store," Stanley said, "And I'll buy it for you." It was as though God had taken me up through the Pearly Gates and said I could

have anything in Heaven, anything at all. In a way, Stanley Ketchel was like a God to me as he was, and still is, thousands of people the world over. He was my brother. So I looked around Heaven and picked out a beautiful red tricycle, and Stan bought it for me and, with me riding ahead of him, we went home together. Next day, after Stan returned to his training quarters, I went riding down a big hill near home. I tripped over the tricycle and broke both my arms. It kept me off the bike for a while but it didn't keep me from worshipping my brother. That's how it's been throughout his career and since his death 51 years ago. Stan's funeral was the biggest in the history of Grand Rapids, Michigan. No mayor, no governor, not even some presidents had a more impressive sendoff than my brother. That's how important he was. I don't have to say so history says it. Between the trip to the big store and Stan's funeral, a lifetime took place, a lifetime that was packed into a few short years. I remember so many things about those years, things that have either been distorted by writers or made up their minds or left out altogether. Still, when a great man dies and becomes a legend, I suppose that is how it usually is. Here are the things I remember. I remember that Stanislaus Steven Kiecal, who was born on September 14th 1887, and changed his name to Stanley Ketchel, was a very warm –hearted, kindly young man, totally different from the murderous renegade some writers tried to make of him. But he could get mighty angry at times! So angry that no one dared come near him. He never learned to pull his punches, and because he could hit so hard, it was very difficult to get sparring partners for him, even though he used 18-ounce gloves. It got so bad they had to furnish special chest protectors for the sparring partners. But even then Stan knocked them down with severe body punches. And once, when he got mad at a trainer, he picked up a big phonograph the boys at the camp were playing and threw it into the lake. He replaced it later, though, with an apology. Stan never stayed mad very long. There are a few mistakes always written about the way he started as a fighter. The truth is that he got the 'fight bug' at the age of 15. At 12 he decided to leave Michigan and go out west and be a cowboy. He had always been a good athlete who could handle himself well in a scrap; but he had no thought of becoming a professional prizefighter until he went west. Mother gave him permission to go, so he hitchhiked as far as Butte, Montana, where he got a job as a bouncer in a lumber camp! At 15 mind you. Well, one night Stan had trouble with three though lumberjacks. He offered to fight all of them at once. The manager of the saloon said, "If you lick these three men, Stan, I'll raise your wages." So Stan knocked them out. He not only got his raise, he got it into his head that he could fight for money. How right he was! The story of his sensational boxing career was correctly reported in Boxing Illustrated. But the story did not do him justice as a man. He was, in fact a loving son to our mother. When he became famous he had mother sell her home in Detroit and took her to live on a farm he bought nine miles north of Grand Rapids. He built a large training camp on the property and lived there himself quite a lot in later years. I remember the place vividly. There I met Wilson Mizner, the famous humorist who was supposed to be Stanley's manager. He wasn't. The only men who ever managed my brother were Willus Britt and Joe O' Conner. Mizner was never more than a close friend. There is no doubt about it - Stan was a ladies man! – And what a man! He loved women and had two large trunks of letters from girls who loved or thought they loved him! I saw the trunks and read many of the letters. One thing about Stan was that he was one of the two handsomest prizefighters in the world when he was active. The other was Joe Thomas. As a testimonial to his marvelous defensive work, he never had a scar, a broken nose or torn eyebrow. He was a gentleman too – as witness the fact that, out of respect to the girls who wrote all those letters, Stanley had them burned. Included in the trunk full of letters were some of his own, in which he described his training. Reading these over and over through the years, I have to marvel at the difference in training methods of my brother and those of present day fighters. And the difference in the kind of fighting is fantastic. Stan used to run well over ten miles a day, and he used to exercise along the way by squeezing a stick. I know because I rode with him in a buggy. In Grand Rapids they still show the tourist the great staircase up a park where Stanley used to run to get his legs in shape. It's the things he did outside of the ring that most people don't know about, including the writers, Things like hanging by his heels from a light tower high over the streets of Grand Rapids; putting sulfur on the street tracks to derail them. Most of these things he did before he became really famous, although he still pulled some boyish stunts after he won the championship. But- there's one thing Stanley never did- drink a lot. Many stories have come down about his being a brutal drunkard, and causing trouble. This is not true! I have been with him more than once when he tossed a twenty dollar gold piece on a bar and ordered drinks for the house. But he himself seldom touched a drop. Quite often he would take me with him on his visits to the big cities, where he was so idolized. On such trips he would always take our uncle along. Uncle would carry Stanley's big diamond ring and the fat bankroll several hundred dollars so that nobody could pick his pocket. I don't know why it sticks to my memory, but whenever Stanley was out in public he wore big Cuban heels, two-and-a half inches high, that made him look taller, although he was all five feet nine inches and weighed 159 pounds. Maybe some smart aleck psychologist knows why, but I don't. And I don't think that's important. As you probably can see, I am not trying to make a real story out of this. I am remembering Stanley Ketchel the man---my brother---and I am putting down the things that come to my mind. I am thinking, for example, of the little known fact that Stanley's hand was broken the time he beat Papke in twenty rounds. And I am thinking of how people said that Stanley always looked so fierce and hard. They didn't know that he didn't want to get his face scarred – so he would bathe in salt brine day after day; this made his skin taut and the flesh very hard, so that he looked grim and fierce. Jim Jeffries did the same. I also think of Stanley's detractors, and how they still say, some of them, that he wasn't as great as the legend says he was. But they don't remember that in 1908 Gentleman Jim Corbett said: "Stanley Ketchel is the best middleweight I ever saw!" Of course Corbett also said he wasn't sure that Stan could lick that sly fox, Jack 'twin' Sullivan. Well, after knocking out Mike in one round, Stan went on to knockout Sullivan's brother Jack in 20 to win the middleweight crown. I think of how it all ended. Maybe I think about that too much. I won't go into it here because it's history. How a farm hand named Walter Dipley accused Stan of insulting his common law wife and shot him in the back. And how Dipley went to a nearby farm, in terror, and asked to be put up for the night. They captured him right away and he didn't put up a struggle; cowards rarely do. More and more I try to think of the happy things about Stan, the good things. About the way he had his first $20 gold piece made into a necklace for our mother; about the way he had expensive cloth put on the walls of the farm instead of wallpaper; it was still on the walls, in good condition, until the old farm burned down a few years ago. I'm still living on the property, and I always will. But as a man lives, so he must die, and the death of Stanley Ketchel is part of his legend. He didn't live like an ordinary man, nor did he act like one. Fifty-one years ago he died, and yet no one is more alive today that my brother Stan. I hope that I helped a little to bring him alive to those who cannot have the honor of knowing him. Many years ago my brother took me into a big department store when I was six. For me it was my conception of Heaven. I hope someday to join him in his.

Ketchel's bothers would grow up to raise families of their own, and Julia and Thomas Ketchel would live an ordinary life after Ketchel's fortune began to wane, until in 1928, tragedy struck the family again. Ketchel's parents were mysteriously found murdered on their farm. Thomas Ketchel's body was found in a hayloft, with his throat cut from ear to ear, and Julia was either shot or stabbed to death inside the house. Their remains would eventually be disinterred and examined for more evidence. However, it was not decided whether the occurrence was a double murder or a murder-suicide. Suspicions circulated within the family that Arthur was not a good person, and had had a role in the killings. But this was never proven. To this day, who was responsible for the killings remains a mystery.

The End

Stanley Ketchel's fighting style was typified by tremendous power, aggression, heart, determination, endless stamina, endurance, a solid chin and extreme courage. At his best, Ketchel possessed an outstanding two-fisted attack, with a tricky shift and a deadly left hook and right cross. Ketchel fooled clever boxers and mauled brute battlers. He had intelligent defensive abilities. Blocking punches well, he exhibited subtle head movements to evade blows and knew how to roll with a punch. He was also one of the masters at picking punches in mid-air, as well as one of the best to parry straight head punches. His creation of angles and constant movement made him a difficult target, and fast footwork and feinting was also part of his repertoire. Yet, he ultimately belonged to the machismo school of fighting, his goal being to seek and destroy.

Ketchel was a thrilling fighter to watch due to his constant offense. He was a remarkable body puncher, leaving opponents little time or opportunity to block his blows, which were rapid and painful. He could unleash so much leather that his foe was kept too busy dodging the artillery to retaliate. However, he was also a dominant force in punch-for-punch battles. He relished matches that would lapse into an endurance contest. Wars that were scheduled for 20, 25 or 45 rounds gave him the opportunity to outlast and out-slug an opponent. He had supreme confidence in his stamina and usually requested fights that spanned nearly two hours. His uncanny talent to fight at an explosive pace and rarely tire amazed his fans and opponents alike.

When Ketchel went berserk in the ring, he stayed berserk. He could both take it and dish it out, and the more he was hurt the worse it got for his opponents. His smoldering rage would keep rising. Yet, occasionally he would pace himself, using his cunning to defeat a opponent, dropping his hands and leaving himself wide open, waiting for the right time to counter his opponent's lead. Once the opponent made his move, Ketchel would parry the punch away, side step or back step out of reach and pop in with left and right counters. He wasn't a silky boxer, but he knew various ways to catch an opponent up, of which the following are three:

1. He would purposely miss a right, quickly step forward with his right foot, and then whip a snapping left-hook or roundhouse punch. The confusing shift and the right swing usually befuddled his adversary, resulting in a full power punch to the mid-section or jaw. Amazingly, Ketchel could use this move so swiftly that his opponent couldn't telegraph where the next punch was coming from.

2. He would move to the left but lead with a fantastic right chop to the chin, followed by a pulverizing left hook.

3. He would fake an attack as a left-hander by darting toward the body, feinting a hook and jumping back out. When his

opponent covered his ribs, Ketchel would quickly switch back to orthodox style and slam a cross or left hook to the chin. Then he would switch back to southpaw again, following with a right, then bringing a left, then bringing a straight right to the face, then bringing a solid right hook or swing to the jaw.

Ketchel put his ring knowledge into operation with crafty execution. But his technique was misunderstood in his own time. To the critics, it made his fighting seem haphazard and amateur. But he would continually emerge victorious from epic fights. Joe Thomas, Billy Papke, Hugo Kelly, Tony Caponi, George Brown, Mike and Jack Sullivan, Frank Klaus, Willie Lewis, Porky Flynn, Sid Lafontise, Philadelphia Jack O' Brian, Sam Langford and Jack Johnson were tremendous athletes who were among his opponents. He was strong enough to fight contending heavyweights and beat them. None of those battles were smooth sailing for Ketchel; every one of them was a brutal struggle. But the power of his fists pulled him through.

About the Author

Manuel Mora is a longtime researcher of current and past boxers, and is especially drawn to Stanley Ketchel for his enigmatic career and even more enigmatic life. In preparation for this book, Mora traveled extensively to access archives that contained information on Ketchel, gaining the permission of periodicals and publishers to reprint pertinent information. Mora currently resides in Webster Groves, MO, a suburb of St. Louis.

My Thanks

To the wonderfully helpful people in Marshfield, MO who allowed my mother, and I to leaf through, and read the large archival ledgers containing the trial transcript testimony of the Stanley Ketchel murder case.
The helpful staff at the library in Conway, MO,
The staff at Grand Rapids City Library,
And to my mother Carliss Mora for her support, and continued belief in the importance of the publication of this book.

My Dedications

I dedicate this book to my late father, Manuel A. Mora II for his insight and suggestion that I should write this book about Stanley Ketchel,
to my friend, the late Mary Ellen Browne, for her encouragement to me while writing this book.
and
to my nephew Nathan Mora, and niece Rachel Mora